KOL HAN'SHAMAH כל הנשמה

CHOIR VOLUME II

ARRANGEMENTS BY
DAVID BERGER, SUSAN LEWIS FRIEDMAN,
RACHELLE NELSON, AND ROBBIE SOLOMON

EDITED BY JOEL EGLASH

companion volume for band also available

TMP
TRANSCONTINENTAL
MUSIC PUBLICATIONS
A Division of the American Conference of Cantors

ABOUT YOUR RIGHT TO REPRODUCE THE MUSIC IN *Kol Han'shamah: Choir Volume II*

Thank you for purchasing this book. *Kol Han'shamah: Choir Volume II* contains choral music and is intended for choirs of varying sizes. **Purchase of this book gives you, the purchaser, the right to reproduce the music in this book for your own ensemble, for use within your community, only.** You may photocopy and distribute a physical copy and/or distribute a digital version of the music in this book to each member of your ensemble. **Purchase of this book also gives you the right to reproduce and distribute the accompanying practice recordings**, solely as a learning tool for your ensemble. The physical and/or digital copies you make and distribute of the music contained in this book may only be used in connection with religious services and for no other purposes. All other rights are reserved to Transcontinental Music Publications. Please report broadcast usages to JLicense.com.

HEBREW PRONUNCIATION GUIDE

VOWELS

a as in father
ai as in aisle (= long i as in island)
e as in bed
ei as in eight (= long a as in ace)
i as in pizza (= long e as in be)
o as in go
u as in lunar
' = unstressed vowel close to ə
or unstressed short e

CONSONANTS

ch as in Bach or
Scottish loch (not as in cheese)
g = hard g as in get (not soft g as in gem)
tz as in boats
h after a vowel is silent
r = like the Italian (rolled) or French r

KOL HAN'SHAMAH: CHOIR VOLUME II

Companion volume to *Kol Han'shamah: Band Volume II* (TMP 994069)

Proofread by Cantor Claire Franco, Dr. Alan Mason, Emily Tummons, and Josh Wiczer
Copyedited by Debra Corman – Music engraved by Josh Wiczer
Design and compositing by Joel Eglash

Transcontinental Music Publications Executive Committee:
—Joel Eglash, Cantor Lauren Phillips Fogelman, Cantor Claire Franco, and Cantor Steven Weiss
American Conference of Cantors: President, Cantor Seth Warner; COO, Rachel Roth
TMP/JLicense Customer Support: Stacey Berliner – TMP/JLicense Production Assistant: Eden Franco

Transcontinental Music Publications / JLicense
A DIVISION OF THE AMERICAN CONFERENCE OF CANTORS
The world's leading publisher of Jewish music since 1938
1375 Remington Road, Suite M – Schaumburg, IL 60173
847.781.7800 – tmp@accantors.org

Printed in the United States of America – 10 9 8 7 6 5 4 3 2 1
Item number 994068 – ISBN 979-8-9889024-1-6
Includes audio download code insert

TranscontinentalMusic.com

Funding and support for *Kol Han'shamah: Choir Volume II*
was generously provided by

The Dr. Jack Gottlieb Memorial Choral Series Fund

and

The Lowell Milken Fund for American Jewish Music
at the UCLA Herb Alpert School of Music

CONTENTS

Each arrangement is presented both in piano-vocal-guitar (PVG) full score and vocal score formats.

Here at Transcontinental Music Publications, the leading publisher of Jewish choral music for a good part of the last hundred years, we have seen an ever-increasing need for easier, reduced-part versions of commonly performed material, including those that existed previously only in SATB format. Many synagogue choirs have become fully volunteer, with fewer trained singers and professionals.

The *Kol Han'shamah: Choir* series was created to provide easy-to-implement two-part choir arrangements of popular tunes for the average volunteer choir. The arrangements in this book were expertly created by Cantor Susan Lewis Friedman (two of hers along with Cantor David Berger), Cantor Rachelle Nelson, and Cantor Robbie Solomon, with these circumstances in mind. For all of these reasons, we launched this new, ongoing series (along with its companion volume, *Kol Han'shamah: Band,* for volunteer synagogue bands) to make available accessible, simpler arrangements without sacrificing good vocal practice or musical quality.

The indispensable rehearsal recordings included with this book feature Cantor Emma Lutz and Cantor Billy Tiep accompanied by Tali Tadmor; our deepest thanks to them for their immense effort and excellent musicianship. For their varied and crucial contributions to this project, thank you to Cantor Claire Franco, Cantor Steven Weiss, Cantor Janice Roger, Emily Tummons, Dr. Alan Mason, the composers and arrangers of the music in and the proofreaders of this volume, Josh Wiczer, and the staff and leadership of the ACC and Transcontinental Music Publications / JLicense, including president Cantor Seth Warner, COO Rachel Roth, and Stacey Berliner. With great thanks we acknowledge the generosity of the Dr. Jack Gottlieb Memorial Choral Series Fund and the Lowell Milken Center for Music of American Jewish Experience at UCLA. In particular, from the Milken and UCLA team, we are grateful to Dr. David Brown, Dr. Mark Kligman, Sharyl Holtzman, Jose Carrillo, and Laura Agudelo Cuartas for use of studio, engineering / mixing / mastering, and resources.

Joel Eglash
Founding Series Editor
Nisan 5784 / April 2024

LEADING A CHOIR: A GUIDE TO USING *KOL HAN'SHAMAH: CHOIR*

by Cantor Janice Roger

Come, let us sing joyously to Adonai. – Psalm 95
Sing to Adonai a new song. – Psalms 96 and 98

THE PSALMIST KNEW THE POWER OF SINGING in the context of worship and advocated for it, not necessarily knowing the other benefits—both physical and mental—of singing and music. How much more, then, is the benefit of singing in a choir? Exponentially more!

A 2010 study conducted by Hebrew Union College–Jewish Institute of Religion and Research Success Technologies (Jerusalem) discovered that singing in a Jewish choral group strengthens Jewish identity and promotes involvement in other Jewish activities. Then there are the benefits to an individual's health and well-being. In his 2018 book *When: The Scientific Secrets of Perfect Timing*, Daniel H. Pink observes that choral singing may be the new exercise. He writes:

> Choral singing calms the heart and boosts endorphin levels. It improves lung function. It increases pain thresholds and reduces the need for pain medication. It also seems to improve your outlook, boosting mood and self-esteem while alleviating feelings of stress and depression.

Our congregational choirs not only add meaning and beauty to prayer, they also benefit each individual in the group. Let your singers know how much you value them and how important they are as "sweet singers of Israel."

The *Kol Han'shamah: Choir* series includes music that is familiar to most of our congregants. The arrangements contained in this book and series are accessible to choirs and leaders with a wide range of abilities, both musically and Judaically. Following are some ideas and tips for working with your choir.

KNOW YOUR CHOIR:

» What is each member's choral experience (congregationally and otherwise)?
» Do they read music?
» How well do they know Hebrew? Have they sung in Hebrew already?
» What is their vocal range? Make sure you write it down for future reference. (By the way, congregants generally sing in the alto/bass range.)

HOW DO I DETERMINE WHO SINGS WHICH PART?

The rule used to be "soprano sings melody." That doesn't work as well for many of the arrangements in this book. Let your choir know that they will not always sing the same part, unlike traditional choral music. Find which voice has the majority of the melody. Put your strongest voices on that part. It will enable the congregation to feel supported. If there is *divisi* (Italian for division) in one of the parts, find one or two singers who can hold their own. That part is optional and not as important as the melody or harmony already provided.

I SEE TWO TREBLE CLEFS AND NO BASS CLEF FOR MEN. DO MEN SING AN OCTAVE LOWER THAN WHAT IS WRITTEN?

Speaking generally, tenors and sopranos will sing the higher part, and altos and basses will sing the lower part. Whichever group they are with, men will sound an octave lower than the women. Some men are used to reading in bass clef; if they can read treble clef, assure them that they can sing an octave lower. If they do not read treble clef, they may learn better by rote (perhaps by listening to the practice track).

WHAT IF I HAVE FEW OR NO MALE VOICES?
When you know the approximate range of each singer, seat those with soprano/tenor range together and those with alto/bass range together. If you have two or more singers in the bass range, you might look for pieces with a three-voice arrangement, putting the lower voices on Voice III. By the way, there are some women who can sing in the tenor/bass range.

ARE THERE WAYS TO HELP MEMBERS WHO DO NOT READ MUSIC?

» There are practice tracks provided with this book. With your purchase, you have the right to distribute them to your community choir members along with the choral scores.
» Encourage familiarity with the song to strengthen the singers' sense of when to enter and exit.
» If a choir member has trouble counting long tacet sections, ask them to include measure counts in their music (for example, 1-2-3-4, 2-2-3-4, etc.).
» If an accompanist or strong reader and separate rooms are available, separate the ensemble and have each part work apart from the other, then bring them together toward the end of the rehearsal.

PLAN YOUR REHEARSAL:

» Having a plan in advance and letting your choristers know about it will help keep everyone focused.
» Have the rehearsal plan visible before the rehearsal begins (on a chalkboard or a piece of paper stuck to the wall). Sending it to them ahead of the rehearsal will allow them time to have their music put in order.
» Begin with physical and vocal warm-ups.
» Mix up music that is familiar with new music throughout the rehearsal.
» Make notes to yourself on how best to rehearse each selection. Notate them (with dates) on your copy of the music.
» Seat voices with similar range together.

A FEW TIPS FOR TEACHING MUSIC TO A CHOIR:

» Have pencils and highlighters available.
» Introduce the song (even if the group knows it from services). Tell singers where the text comes from, what it means, its place in the service, and something about the composer or folk origin.
» Once you determine who is singing which voice, have the singers mark their part.
» Sing through the melody so that the group hears it accurately.
» Talk through the roadmap of the music—make sure everyone knows where to go if there is a refrain that is notated only once.
» Teach the refrain first, to build confidence in that section, or begin with the most difficult section so the rest seems easier.
» Try mixing things up by teaching the text from the last phrase to the first.

Here is a method that generally works to rehearse choral music. Try working on the piece phrase-by-phrase as follows:

1. Read Hebrew in rhythm of music (use the echo technique for accuracy);

2. Sing the melody voice for the phrase, then have singers on that part repeat;
3. Do the above two steps for the other voice;
4. Combine voices and repeat several times.

If the text/music combination appears in other places in the arrangement, you could find those places and have the groups sing them once they are learned.

Thank you for continuing the tradition of singing Jewish choral music. By leading your choir, you are doing important work that benefits both your congregation and the singers in your group. The composers, arrangers, editors, and I hope this volume will make your sacred task easier.

B'hatzlacha—to your success,

Cantor Janice Roger
Nisan 5784 / April 2024

ABOUT THE ARRANGEMENTS OF *KOL HAN'SHAMAH: CHOIR VOLUME II*

Adon Olam (Traditional)
This setting is a congregational favorite and always brings a smile to nearly everyone. People have often told me that it takes them back to their camp days, and they always participate. This setting spells out the echo/call and response which is popular in its congregational singing. I recommend swinging the eighth notes, both in the voice and accompaniment, but it is written with just straight eighths so that it is easier for those who are not fluent music readers in a volunteer choir to sing. I also used an easy harmony of thirds, coming back together in unison to punctuate the important refrain text of "Adon Olam," signifying that we all together worship the One God of the world. —Susan Lewis Friedman, arranger

Ahavat Olam (Eric Mandell)
"Ahavat Olam" has always felt like a gentle waltz to me. Therefore, I arranged the piano accompaniment with a 6/8 meter rather than a 3/4 meter. Though this is written as a duet, all of my arrangements can be sung with a solo voice. I realize that many congregations do not have the ability to have more than one singer. For those who can add an additional voice, you will note that I use ornamentation and embellishments to make the melody sound more fluid and interesting. —Rachelle Nelson, arranger

Bar'chu (Rachelle Nelson)
"Bar'chu" was written during my years in cantorial school. My rabbi at that time was a yeshivah graduate who was very musical, with a love for Chasidic music. I wanted to create that same feeling in the "Bar'chu" and so I composed it with a 3/4 meter and a dance-like rhythm. I hope you will sing it with lots of joy. —Rachelle Nelson, arranger

L'chah Dodi (Aaron Bensoussan)
Like many examples of Sephardic settings, Bensoussan's "L'chah Dodi" articulates the *shva* where it appears in many words (e.g., li-<u>ke</u>-rat kalah). This gives a more rhythmic feel to the arrangement.
—Robbie Solomon, arranger

Light One Candle (Peter Yarrow)
When writing this arrangement, as with most of my arrangements, I tried to write the harmony which I would naturally sing by ear, but making modifications that would work for my volunteer choir. The message is powerful, and I have found that using quarter-note triplets is very effective. I recommend conducting each one of them for the choir, so that they are sure to get the rhythm. David Berger has included a beautiful use of passing the melody back and forth between the parts, as well as another optional part in the small notes. —Susan Lewis Friedman, arranger

Mi Chamochah (Dan Nichols and Mason Cooper)
I love singing harmony on this setting with my b'nai mitzvah students and I was excited to write it! I particularly love singing the suspensions. It's so fun to echo "t'hilot" and "feleh," and it often comes with hand motions too, which I highly recommend doing, especially if you are using this version with a youth choir. It is very rhythmic, and I tried to be very intentional in the arrangement so that it will be clear to singers of all musical levels in how to execute the rhythm. —Susan Lewis Friedman, arranger

Mi Shebeirach (Debbie Friedman)
Jeff Klepper made a beautiful unpublished four-part arrangement of this which both of my volunteer choirs have used for decades. I was inspired by some of the elements in this arrangement when I wrote this two-part version. David Berger made some beautiful additions of handing off the text from one part to the other, and when we get to the heart of the prayer, our bequest for "the renewal of body, the renewal of spirit," we come together in unison for a very powerful moment. This moment is augmented by the somewhat countrapuntal writing David used in the verses. —Susan Lewis Friedman, arranger

Olam Chesed Yibaneh (Menachem Creditor)
"Olam Chesed Yibaneh" is filled with soul. If you sing it without grasping the Jewish soul, it won't work. I arranged the melody so that it could build and build just like a *nigun* and then descend once again. You can sing the song with the words or just close your eyes and let the melody lift you to another place. I pray that you take the congregation with you on this spiritual and soulful ride. Take your time in building the melody. —Rachelle Nelson, arranger

Oseh Shalom (Elana Jagoda)
This setting is a favorite of my religious school students and people always sing along with it. It is very rhythmic, which is a trademark of my own singing, playing, and writing, and I wanted to be intentional in writing it so that the rhythms would be sung as correctly as possible because when they are, it's very fun (especially when it is being accompanied by guitar). Often, the parts move in opposite directions, representing our different individual ways that we all find peace in our lives. It has an optional solo in the last few bars which is effective but simple enough for a volunteer or professional musical leader to sing.
—Susan Lewis Friedman, arranger

Shalom Aleichem (Sol Zim)
In this Chasidic-style setting of the Shabbat table song which opens and closes many Friday night services, Zim uses a *nigun* with a strong two-beat rhythm. Teach your congregation to clap on the off-beat.
—Robbie Solomon, arranger

Shalom Rav (Jeff Klepper and Dan Freelander)
My first introduction to Jeff Klepper was in cantorial school and then in a very small studio in Flatbush where I played flute on one of the first of Kol B'Seder albums. I have always heard a sustaining bass in parts of the song while the right hand moves in different positions within the same chord. Then, in the C section, I wrote a more commanding accompaniment to define what the words were saying. Klepper/Freelander's "Shalom Rav" has become a classic in synagogues throughout the world.
—Rachelle Nelson, arranger

Shir Chadash (Julie Silver)
"A new song unto God." Julie Silver's setting resonates with joy and energy, leading up to the long held note at the end of each repeat. Vocally develop that note as it cycles through the four chords.
—Robbie Solomon, arranger

Y'did Nefesh (Ehud and Sarah Zweig)
A love song to Shabbat, the Zweigs' music swells in 3/4 time to emphasize our devotion.
—Robbie Solomon, arranger

Yih'yu L'ratzon (Hollis Schachner)
"Yih'yu L'ratzon" is one of my favorites. The music was composed by Hollis Schachner who I was mentoring many moons ago. I remember coming into my office one day and Hollis was sitting at my piano with a song that she had written. I loved it immediately and sat down to add a second voice and accompaniment. Her "Yih'yu L'ratzon" is now one of the most beloved songs in the Reform cantorate today. —Rachelle Nelson, arranger

Yism'chu (Traditional Chasidic)
This old favorite can be performed without accompaniment as it has been for years in more traditional synagogues. The B section is done freely (without rhythm) with an optional call and answer background.
—Robbie Solomon, arranger

TRACK LIST FOR ACCOMPANYING ALBUM

ADON OLAM
Traditional, arr. Susan Lewis Friedman
1. Master Track
2. Master Track with band
3. Part I Practice Track
4. Part II Practice Track

AHAVAT OLAM
Eric Mandell, arr. Rachelle Nelson
5. Master Track
6. Master Track with band
7. Part I Practice Track
8. Part II Practice Track

BAR'CHU
Rachelle Nelson, arr. Rachelle Nelson
9. Master Track
10. Master Track with band
11. Part I Practice Track
12. Part II Practice Track

L'CHAH DODI
Aaron Bensoussan, arr. Robbie Solomon
13. Master Track
14. Master Track with band
15. Part I Practice Track
16. Part II Practice Track

LIGHT ONE CANDLE
Peter Yarrow, arr. Susan Lewis Friedman and David Berger
17. Master Track
18. Master Track with band
19. Part I Practice Track
20. Part II Practice Track

MI CHAMOCHAH
Dan Nichols and Mason Cooper, arr. Susan Lewis Friedman
21. Master Track
22. Master Track with band
23. Part I Practice Track
24. Part II Practice Track

MI SHEBEIRACH
Debbie Friedman, arr. Susan Lewis Friedman and David Berger
25. Master Track
26. Master Track with band
27. Part I Practice Track
28. Part II Practice Track

OLAM CHESED YIBANEH
Menachem Creditor, arr. Rachelle Nelson
29. Master Track
30. Master Track with band
31. Part I Practice Track
32. Part II Practice Track

OSEH SHALOM
Elana Jagoda, arr. Susan Lewis Friedman
33. Master Track
34. Master Track with band
35. Part I Practice Track
36. Part II Practice Track

SHALOM ALEICHEM
Sol Zim, arr. Robbie Solomon
37. Master Track
38. Master Track with band
39. Part I Practice Track
40. Part II Practice Track

SHALOM RAV
Jeff Klepper and Dan Freelander, arr. Rachelle Nelson
41. Master Track
42. Master Track with band
43. Part I Practice Track
44. Part II Practice Track

SHIR CHADASH
Julie Silver, arr. Robbie Solomon
45. Master Track
46. Master Track with band
47. Part I Practice Track
48. Part II Practice Track

Y'DID NEFESH
Ehud and Sarah Zweig, arr. Robbie Solomon
49. Master Track
50. Master Track with band
51. Part I Practice Track
52. Part II Practice Track

YIH'YU L'RATZON
Hollis Schachner, arr. Rachelle Nelson
53. Master Track
54. Master Track with band
55. Part I Practice Track
56. Part II Practice Track

YISM'CHU
Traditional Chasidic, arr. Robbie Solomon
57. Master Track
58. Master Track with band
59. Part I Practice Track
60. Part II Practice Track

Vocals: **Cantor Emma Lutz** and **Cantor Billy Tiep**; Piano: **Tali Tadmor**.
Violin: **Rebecca Beerstein**; Clarinet: **Jacob Freiman**; Trumpet: **Remy Ohara**; Bass: **Skyler Lee**.
Produced by Joel Eglash; engineered by Laura Agudelo Cuartas. Recorded April 2024 at UCLA Herb Alpert School of Music Studio, Los Angeles, California. Mixed and mastered by Jose Carrillo and Joel Eglash. Recordings sponsored by and coordinated with the Lowell Milken Center for Music of American Jewish Experience (UCLA) (Dr. Mark Kligman, Dr. David Brown, and Sharyl Holtzman). Instrumentalists performed in cooperation with UCLA Herb Alpert School of Music.

KOL HAN'SHAMAH כל הנשמה

CHOIR VOLUME II

Adon Olam

אדון עולם

Text: **Liturgy**

Music: Traditional

Arranged by **Susan Lewis Friedman**
Piano arranged by **Susan Lewis Friedman** and **Gregory Shifrin**
Corresponding band arrangement by **Emily Tummons**

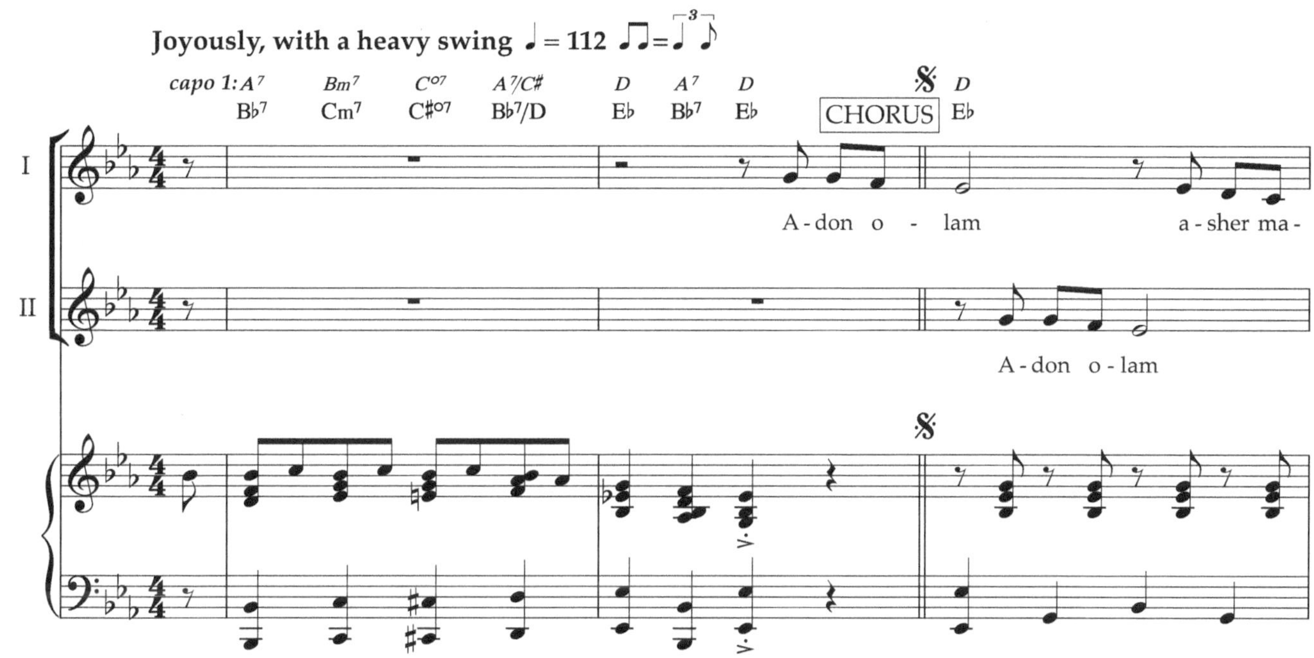

Corresponding band arrangement available in *Kol Han'shamah: Band Volume II* (TMP 994069)

Last time to Coda
I
II
kol, a - zai Me-lech sh'-mo nik-ra, a - don o - lam. 1. V' - 2. V' - 3. V' -
v'-chef-tzo kol a - zai Me-lech sh'-mo nik-ra, a - don o - lam.
VERSES
a - cha - rei kich-lot ha - kol, l'-va-do yim-loch no-ra, a-don o - lam. V'-
hu e - chad v'-ein shei - ni, l'-ham-shil lo l'-hach-bi-rah, a-don o - lam. B'-
hu Ei - li v'-chai go - a - li, v'-tzur chev-li b'-eit tza-rah, a-don o - lam. V'-
4. B' - ya - do af-kid ru - chi, b'-eit i-shan v'-a-i-rah, a-don o - lam. V'-
1. V'-a - cha - rei kich-lot ha-kol l'-va-do yim-loch no-ra, a-don o - lam.
2. V'-hu e - chad v'-ein shei-ni, l'-ham-shil lo l'-hach-bi-rah, a-don o - lam.
3. V'-hu Ei - li v'-chai go-a-li v'-tzur chev-li b'-eit tza-rah, a-don o - lam.
4. B' - ya - do af-kid ru-chi, b'-eit i-shan v'-a-i-rah, a-don o - lam.

Em A7 Em A7 A A7/C# D A7 D
Fm Bb7 Fm Bb7 Bb Bb7/D Eb Bb7 Eb
1.-3. D.S.
4. D.S. al Coda
I
hu ha - yah, v' - hu ho - veh, v' - hu yih'-yeh, b' - tif - a - rah, a - don o - lam. A - don o -
li rei - shit b' - li tach - lit, v' - lo ha - oz v' - ha - mis - rah, a - don o - lam. A - don o -
hu ni - si u - ma - nos li, m' - nat ko - si b'-yom ek - ra, a - don o - lam. A - don o -
im ru - chi g' - vi - ya - ti, A - do - nai li v' - lo i - ra, a - don o - lam. A - don o -
II
V' - hu ha - yah, v' - hu ho - veh, v' - hu yih'-yeh, b' - tif - a - rah, a - don o - lam.
B' - li rei - shit b' - li tach - lit, v' - lo ha - oz v' - ha - mis - rah, a - don o - lam.
V' - hu ni - si u - ma - nos li, m' - nat ko - si b'-yom ek - ra, a - don o - lam.
V' - im ru - chi g' - vi - ya - ti, A - do - nai li v' - lo i - ra, a - don o - lam.
1.-3. D.S.
4. D.S. al Coda

CODA

A7 D A7 D
Bb7 Eb Bb7 Eb
I
non-rit.
zai Me - lech sh' - mo nik - ra, a - don o - lam.
II
non-rit.
zai Me - lech sh' - mo nik - ra, a - don o - lam.
non-rit.

You are our Eternal God,
who reigned before any being had been created;
when all was done according to Your will,
then You were called Ruler.

אֲדוֹן עוֹלָם אֲשֶׁר מָלַךְ,
בְּטֶרֶם כָּל יְצִיר נִבְרָא.
לְעֵת נַעֲשָׂה בְחֶפְצוֹ כֹּל,
אֲזַי מֶלֶךְ שְׁמוֹ נִקְרָא.

And after all ceases to be,
You alone will rule in majesty.
You have been, are yet,
and will be in glory.

וְאַחֲרֵי כִּכְלוֹת הַכֹּל,
לְבַדּוֹ יִמְלוֹךְ נוֹרָא.
וְהוּא הָיָה, וְהוּא הֹוֶה,
וְהוּא יִהְיֶה, בְּתִפְאָרָה.

And You are One;
none other can compare to or consort with You.
You are without beginning, without end.
To You belong power and dominion.

וְהוּא אֶחָד וְאֵין שֵׁנִי,
לְהַמְשִׁיל לוֹ לְהַחְבִּירָה.
בְּלִי רֵאשִׁית בְּלִי תַכְלִית,
וְלוֹ הָעֹז וְהַמִּשְׂרָה.

And You are my God, my living Redeemer,
my Rock in times of trouble and distress.
You are my standard bearer and my refuge,
my benefactor when I call on You.

וְהוּא אֵלִי וְחַי גֹּאֲלִי,
וְצוּר חֶבְלִי בְּעֵת צָרָה.
וְהוּא נִסִּי וּמָנוֹס לִי,
מְנָת כּוֹסִי בְּיוֹם אֶקְרָא.

Into Your hands I entrust my spirit,
when I sleep and when I wake,
and with my spirit my body also;
Adonai is with me and I shall not fear.

בְּיָדוֹ אַפְקִיד רוּחִי,
בְּעֵת אִישַׁן וְאָעִירָה.
וְעִם רוּחִי גְּוִיָּתִי,
יְיָ לִי וְלֹא אִירָא.

Adon Olam

אדון עולם

Text: **Liturgy**

Music: Traditional

Arranged by **Susan Lewis Friedman**
Piano arranged by **Susan Lewis Friedman** and **Gregory Shifrin**
Corresponding band arrangement by **Emily Tummons**

Corresponding band arrangement available in *Kol Han'shamah: Band Volume II* (TMP 994069)

12
I
lot ha - kol, l' - va-do yim-loch no-ra, a-don o-lam. V'-hu ha-yah, v'-
ein shei - ni, l'-ham-shil lo l'-hach-bi-rah, a-don o-lam. B'-li rei-shit b'-
chai go - a - li, v'-tzur chev-li b'-eit tza-rah, a-don o-lam. V'-hu ni - si u-
kid ru - chi, b'-eit i-shan v'-a-i-rah, a-don o-lam. V'-im ru-chi g'-
II
rei kich-lot ha-kol l'-va-do yim-loch no-ra, a-don o-lam. V'-hu ha-
chad v'-ein shei-ni, l'-ham-shil lo l'-hach-bi-rah, a-don o-lam. B'-li rei-
li v'-chai go-a-li v'-tzur chev-li b'-eit tza-rah, a-don o-lam. V'-hu ni-
do af-kid ru-chi, b'-eit i-shan v'-a-i-rah, a-don o-lam. V'-im ru-

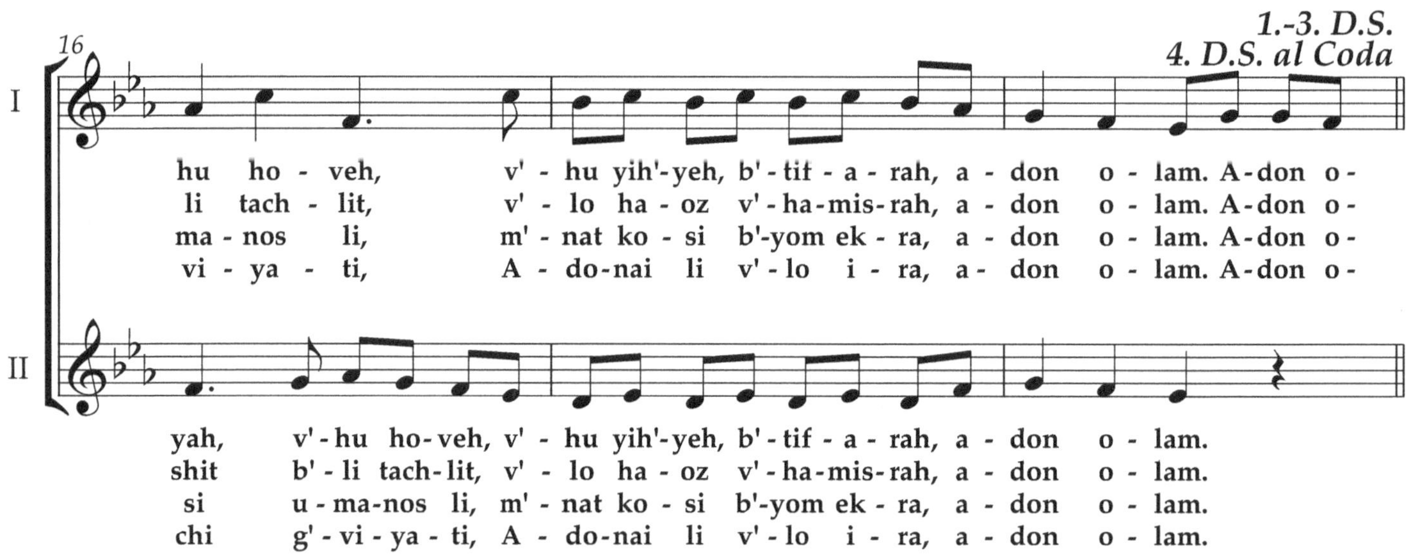
16
1.-3. D.S.
4. D.S. al Coda
I
hu ho - veh, v'-hu yih'-yeh, b'-tif-a-rah, a-don o-lam. A-don o-
li tach - lit, v'-lo ha-oz v'-ha-mis-rah, a-don o-lam. A-don o-
ma - nos li, m'-nat ko-si b'-yom ek-ra, a-don o-lam. A-don o-
vi - ya - ti, A-do-nai li v'-lo i-ra, a-don o-lam. A-don o-
II
yah, v'-hu ho-veh, v'-hu yih'-yeh, b'-tif-a-rah, a-don o-lam.
shit b'-li tach-lit, v'-lo ha-oz v'-ha-mis-rah, a-don o-lam.
si u-ma-nos li, m'-nat ko-si b'-yom ek-ra, a-don o-lam.
chi g'-vi-ya-ti, A-do-nai li v'-lo i-ra, a-don o-lam.

CODA

19
I
non-rit.
zai Me-lech sh'-mo nik-ra, a-don o-lam.
II
non-rit.
zai Me-lech sh'-mo nik-ra, a-don o-lam.

Ahavat Olam

אהבת עולם

Text: **Evening liturgy**

Music: **Eric Mandell**

Arranged by **Rachelle Nelson**
Corresponding band arrangement by **Emily Tummons**

Corresponding band arrangement available in *Kol Han'shamah: Band Volume II* (TMP 994069)

10
Em B Em E7 Am D D7 G
I
ta. Al kein, A-do-nai E-lo-hei-nu, b'-shoch-bei-nu u-v-ku-mei-nu na-
II
ta. Al kein, A-do-nai E-lo-hei-nu, b'-shoch-bei-nu u-v-ku-mei-nu na-
15
Cmaj7 D7 G B7 Em E7 Am
si-ach, b'-chu-ke-cha, v'-nis-mach b'-div-rei To-ra-te-cha
si-ach, b'-chu-ke-cha, v'-nis-mach b'-div-rei To-ra-te-cha
19
D D7 G Cmaj7 B7 Em
u-v-mitz-vo-te-cha l'-o-lam va-ed. Ki
u-v-mitz-vo-te-cha l'-o-lam va-ed. Ki

Everlasting love
You offered Your people Israel
by teaching us Torah and mitzvot,
laws and precepts.
Therefore, Adonai our God,
when we lie down and when we rise up,
we will meditate on Your laws
and Your commandments.
We will rejoice in Your Torah forever.
Day and night we will reflect on them
for they are our life and doing them lengthen our days.

אַהֲבַת עוֹלָם
בֵּית יִשְׂרָאֵל עַמְּךָ אָהָבְתָּ,
תּוֹרָה וּמִצְוֹת,
חֻקִּים וּמִשְׁפָּטִים, אוֹתָנוּ לִמַּדְתָּ.
עַל כֵּן, יְיָ אֱלֹהֵינוּ,
בְּשָׁכְבֵנוּ וּבְקוּמֵנוּ
נָשִׂיחַ בְּחֻקֶּיךָ,
וְנִשְׂמַח בְּדִבְרֵי תוֹרָתֶךָ
וּבְמִצְוֹתֶיךָ לְעוֹלָם וָעֶד.
כִּי הֵם חַיֵּינוּ וְאֹרֶךְ יָמֵינוּ,
וּבָהֶם נֶהְגֶּה יוֹמָם וָלָיְלָה.

Ahavat Olam

אהבת עולם

Text: **Evening liturgy**

Music: **Eric Mandell**

Arranged by **Rachelle Nelson**
Corresponding band arrangement by **Emily Tummons**

Corresponding band arrangement available in *Kol Han'shamah: Band Volume II* (TMP 994069)

14
I
mei - nu na - si- ach, b'-chu-ke - cha, v'-nis-mach b'-div-rei To - ra -
II
mei - nu na - si- ach, b'-chu-ke - cha, v'-nis-mach b'-div-rei To - ra -
18
I
te - cha u - v-mitz - vo - te - cha l'-o - lam va - ed. Ki
II
te - cha u - v-mitz - vo - te - cha l'-o - lam va - ed. Ki
C
23
I
heim cha - yei - nu v' - o - rech ya - mei - nu u - va-
II
heim cha - yei - nu v' - o - rech ya - mei - nu u - va-
27
I
rit.
hem neh - geh yo - mam va - lai - lah.
II
rit.
hem neh - geh yo - mam va - lai - lah.

Bar'chu ברכו

Text: **Liturgy**

Music: **Rachelle Nelson**

Piano arranged by **Rachelle Nelson** and **Gregory Shifrin**
Corresponding band arrangement by **Emily Tummons**

Corresponding band arrangement available in *Kol Han'shamah: Band Volume II* (TMP 994069)

13
Am Dm
D G
D/F# G/B
F(add9) B♭(add9)
G C
I
Yai lai lai lai lai lai lai, lai lai lai lai lai lai
II
Yai lai lai lai lai lai lai, lai lai lai lai lai lai
III
optional
Yai lai lai lai lai lai lai, lai lai
19
Am Dm
G/A C/D
Am Dm
G7 C7
B
C F
G C
E A
E7 A7
lai. Lai lai lai lai lai lai lai lai lai lai lai lai lai
tutti
lai. Lai lai lai lai lai lai lai lai lai lai lai lai lai
lai.

25
F G C G7 C
B♭ C F C7 F
I
lai lai lai lai lai lai. Lai lai lai lai lai lai lai
II
lai lai lai lai lai lai. Lai lai lai lai lai lai lai lai lai
31
G E E7 F G Em7 Am G/A Am G/A
C A A7 B♭ C Am7 Dm C/D Dm C/D
I
lai lai lai lai lai lai lai lai lai.
II
lai lai lai lai lai lai lai lai lai lai lai lai lai.

C
37
Am Dm
D G
D/F# G/B
F(add9) B♭(add9)
G C
solo
I
II
Ba - r' - chu et A - do - nai ha - m - vo -
43
Am Dm
G/A C/D
Am Dm
G7 C7
C F
G C
E A
E7 A7
tutti
rach!
Ba - ruch A - do - nai ha - m - vo - rach
Ba - ruch A - do - nai ha - m - vo - rach
49
F B♭
G C
C F
G7 C7
C F
l' - o - lam va - ed. Ba - ruch A - do - nai
l' - o - lam va - ed.

55
G C E A E7 A7 F B♭ G C Em7 Am7 Am Dm G/A C/D Am Dm G/A C/D
I
ha - m - vo - rach l' - o - lam va - ed!
II
61
D
Am Dm D G D/F# G/B F(add9) B♭(add9)
Lai lai lai lai lai lai lai, lai lai lai
Lai lai lai lai lai lai lai, lai lai lai
66
G C Am Dm G/A C/D Am Dm G/A C/D Am Dm
lai lai lai lai. Yai lai lai
lai lai lai lai. Yai lai lai
III
Yai lai lai

Praise Adonai to whom praise is due forever!
Praised be Adonai to whom praise is due, now and forever!

בָּרְכוּ אֶת יְיָ הַמְבֹרָךְ!
בָּרוּךְ יְיָ הַמְבֹרָךְ לְעוֹלָם וָעֶד!

Bar'chu

ברכו

Text: **Liturgy**

Music: **Rachelle Nelson**

Piano arranged by **Rachelle Nelson** and **Gregory Shifrin**
Corresponding band arrangement by **Emily Tummons**

Corresponding band arrangement available in *Kol Han'shamah: Band Volume II* (TMP 994069)

21
B
I
lai lai lai lai lai lai lai lai lai lai lai lai lai lai lai lai lai lai.
II
lai lai lai lai lai lai lai lai lai lai lai lai lai lai lai lai lai lai.
28
I
Lai lai lai lai lai lai lai lai lai lai lai lai lai lai lai
II
Lai lai lai lai lai lai lai lai lai lai lai lai lai lai lai lai lai lai lai lai lai lai
35
C
solo
I
lai. Ba - r' - chu et A - do - nai ha - m - vo - rach!
II
lai.
44
tutti
I
Ba - ruch A - do - nai ha - m - vo - rach l' - o - lam va - ed.
II
Ba - ruch A - do - nai ha - m - vo - rach l' - o - lam va - ed.

52
I
Ba - ruch A - do - nai ha - m - vo - rach l' - o - lam va - ed!
II
60
D
I
Lai lai lai lai lai lai lai, lai lai lai lai lai lai lai.
optional divisi
II
Lai lai lai lai lai lai lai, lai lai lai lai lai lai lai.
69
rit.
I
Yai lai lai lai lai lai lai, lai lai lai lai lai lai lai.
II
Yai lai lai lai lai lai lai, lai lai lai lai lai lai lai.
III
Yai lai lai lai lai lai lai, lai lai lai.

L'chah Dodi

לכה דודי

Text: **Shlomo Alkabetz ben HaLevi (16th C.)**

Music: **Aaron Bensoussan**

Arranged by **Robbie Solomon**
Corresponding band arrangement by **Emily Tummons**

Corresponding band arrangement available in *Kol Han'shamah: Band Volume II* (TMP 994069)

B
8
Em Am7 B7 F#m7(b5) B7 Em B7
I
chah do-di li - k-rat ka-lah, p'-nei Shab-bat n'-ka - b'-lah. L'-
II
chah do-di, p' - nei Shab-bat n'-ka - b'-lah. L'-chah, l'-
12
Em Am7 B F#m7(b5) B F#m7(b5) B7 Em D
chah do-di li - k-rat ka-lah, p'-nei Shab-bat n'-ka - b'-lah. 1. Sha - 2. Lik - 5. Hit -
chah do-di, p' - nei Shab-bat n' - ka-b'-lah. 1. Sha - 2. Lik - 5. Hit -
C
16
G Am D Am B7
mor v'-za-chor b'-di-bur e-chad, hish-mi-a - nu Eil
rat Shab-bat l'-chu v'-neil'-chah, ki hi m'-kor ha-
o - r'-ri, hit - o - r'-ri, ki va o-reich,
mor v'-za-chor, hish-mi - a - nu,
rat Shab-bat, ki hi m'-kor,
o - r'-ri, hit - o - r'-ri,

19
Em D G Am D
I
ham' - yu-chad, A-do-nai e-chad u-sh-mo e-chad,
b'ra - chah, mei-rosh mi-ke - dem n'-su - chah,
ku-mi o - ri, u - ri u - - ri shir da-bei - ri,
II
A-do-nai e-chad, l' -
mei-rosh mi-ke - dem, sof
u - ri u - ri
22
1.2. Am F♯m7(♭5) B B7 Em
3. Am F♯m7(♭5) B
I
l'-sheim ul-tif-e - ret v'-li-t-hi-lah. L'- k'vod A-do-nai a -
sof ma-a-seh b'-macha-sha-vah t'chi-lah. L'-
II
sheim ul-tif-e - ret v'-li-t-hi-lah. L'- k'vod A-do-nai a -
ma - a-seh b'-macha-sha-vah t'chi-lah. L'-

25
B7 Em D Em Am7 B F#m7(b5) B7
I
la - yich nig - lah. L' - chah do - di li - k-rat ka - lah, p' - nei Shab - bat
II
la - yich nig - lah. L' - chah do - di, p' - nei Shab - bat
29
Em Am7 B F#m7(b5) B7 F#m7(b5) B7 Em
I
n'-ka - b'- lah. L' - chah do - di li - k-rat ka - lah, p'-nei Shab - bat n' - ka - b'- lah.
II
n'-ka - b'- lah. L' - chah, l' - chah do - di, p' - nei Shab - bat n' - ka - b'- lah.
34
E Em D C B7
I
Ya la lai lai, ya la lai lai, ya la lai lai, la la lai lai
II
Ya la lai lai, ya la lai lai, ya la lai lai, la la lai lai

36
Em D C B Em D7
poco rit.
Piu lento
I
lai, ya la lai___ lai, ya la lai___ lai, ya la lai___ lai, la la lai lai lai. 9. Bo -
II
lai, ya la lai___ lai, ya la lai___ lai, ya la lai___ lai, la la lai lai lai. 9. Bo -
39
F
G Am D7 Am B7 Em D G
I
i v'-sha-lom a - te - ret ba - lah,___ gam b'-sim-chah uv - tzo - ho-lah,
II
i v'-sha-lom___ a - te - ret ba - lah,___ gam b'-sim-chah___ uv - tzo-ho-lah,
43
Am D7 Am7 B7 Tempo I Em
I
toch e-mu-nei am s'-gu - lah,___ bo - i cha-lah, bo - i cha-lah. L'-
II
toch e-mu-nei___ am s'-gu - lah, bo - i cha-lah, bo - i___ cha-lah. L'-
Tempo I

47
G
Em Am7 B F#m7(b5) B7 Em
I
chah do-di li - k-rat ka-lah, p'-nei Shab-bat n'-ka - b'-lah. L'-
II
chah do-di, p' - nei Shab-bat n'-ka - b'-lah. L'-chah, l'-
51
Am7 B F#m7(b5) B7 F#m7(b5) B7 Em
I
chah do-di li - k-rat ka-lah, p'-nei Shab-bat n' - ka - b'-lah.
II
chah do-di, p' - nei Shab-bat n' - ka-b'-lah.

Beloved, come to meet the bride; beloved, come to greet Shabbat.	לְכָה דוֹדִי לִקְרַאת כַּלָּה, פְּנֵי שַׁבָּת נְקַבְּלָה.
1. "Keep" and "remember": a single command the Only God caused us to hear; the Eternal is One, God's name is One; glory and praise are God's.	1. שָׁמוֹר וְזָכוֹר בְּדִבּוּר אֶחָד, הִשְׁמִיעָנוּ אֵל הַמְיֻחָד, יְיָ אֶחָד וּשְׁמוֹ אֶחָד, לְשֵׁם וּלְתִפְאֶרֶת וְלִתְהִלָּה.
2. Come with me to meet Shabbat, forever a fountain of blessing. Still it flows, as from the start: the last of days, for which the first was made.	2. לִקְרַאת שַׁבָּת לְכוּ וְנֵלְכָה, כִּי הִיא מְקוֹר הַבְּרָכָה, מֵרֹאשׁ מִקֶּדֶם נְסוּכָה, סוֹף מַעֲשֶׂה בְּמַחֲשָׁבָה תְּחִלָּה.
5. Awake, awake, your light has come! Arise, shine, awake, and sing: the Eternal's glory dawns upon you.	5. הִתְעוֹרְרִי, הִתְעוֹרְרִי, כִּי בָא אוֹרֵךְ, קוּמִי אוֹרִי, עוּרִי עוּרִי, שִׁיר דַּבֵּרִי, כְּבוֹד יְיָ עָלַיִךְ נִגְלָה.
9. Enter in peace, O crown of your husband; enter in gladness, enter in joy. Come to the people that keeps its faith. Enter, O bride! Enter, O bride!	9. בּוֹאִי בְשָׁלוֹם עֲטֶרֶת בַּעְלָהּ, גַּם בְּשִׂמְחָה וּבְצָהֳלָה, תּוֹךְ אֱמוּנֵי עַם סְגֻלָּה, בּוֹאִי כַלָּה, בּוֹאִי כַלָּה.

L'chah Dodi

לכה דודי

Text: **Shlomo Alkabetz ben HaLevi (16th C.)**

Music: **Aaron Bensoussan**

Arranged by **Robbie Solomon**
Corresponding band arrangement by **Emily Tummons**

Corresponding band arrangement available in *Kol Han'shamah: Band Volume II* (TMP 994069)

B
8
I
II
chah do-di li-k-rat ka-lah, p'-nei Shab-bat n'-ka-b'-lah. L'-
chah do-di, p'-nei Shab-bat n'-ka-b'-lah. L'-chah, l'-
12
chah do-di li-k-rat ka-lah, p'-nei Shab-bat n'-ka - b'-lah. 1. Sha- 2. Lik- 5. Hit-
chah do-di, p'-nei Shab-bat n'-ka-b'-lah. 1. Sha- 2. Lik- 5. Hit-
C
16
mor v'-za-chor b'-di-bur e-chad, hish-mi-a-nu Eil
rat Shab-bat l'-chu v'-neil'-chah, ki hi m'-kor ha-
o - r'-ri, hit-o - r'-ri, ki va o-reich,
mor v'-za-chor, hish-mi-a - nu,
rat Shab-bat, ki hi m'-kor,
o - r'-ri, hit-o - r'-ri,
19
ham' - yu-chad, A-do-nai e-chad u-sh-mo e-chad,
b'ra - chah, mei-rosh mi-ke - dem n'-su - chah,
ku-mi o - ri, u - ri u - ri shir da-bei - ri,
A-do-nai e-chad, l'-
mei-rosh mi-ke-dem, sof
u - ri u - ri

22
1.2.
3.
I
l'-sheim ul-tif-e - ret v' - li - t - hi - lah. L'- k'vod A-do-nai a-
sof ma-a-seh b'-macha-sha-vah t'chi-lah. L'-
II
sheim ul-tif-e - ret v' - li - t - hi - lah. L'- k'vod A-do-nai a-
ma - a-seh b'-macha-sha-vah t'chi-lah. L'-
25
D
I
la-yich nig - lah. L' - chah do-di li - k-rat ka-lah, p'-nei Shab-bat
II
la-yich nig - lah. L' - chah do-di, p' - nei Shab-bat
29
I
n' - ka - b'- lah. L' - chah do - di li - k-rat ka-lah,
II
n' - ka - b'- lah. L'-chah, l' - chah do - di, p' -
32
E
I
p'-nei Shab-bat n' - ka - b'-lah. Ya la lai lai, ya la lai
II
nei Shab-bat n' - ka-b'-lah. Ya la lai lai, ya la lai

35
I
lai, ya la lai lai, la la lai lai lai, ya la lai lai, ya la lai
II
lai, ya la lai lai, la la lai lai lai, ya la lai lai, ya la lai
37
poco rit.
Piu lento
F
lai, ya la lai lai, la la lai lai lai. 9. Bo - i v'-sha-lom a -
lai, ya la lai lai, la la lai lai lai. 9. Bo - i v'-sha-lom a -
40
te-ret ba - lah, gam b'-sim-chah uv - tzo - ho-lah, toch e-mu-nei
te-ret ba - lah, gam b'-sim-chah uv - tzo-ho-lah, toch e-mu-nei
44
Tempo I
G
am s'-gu - lah, bo-i cha-lah, bo-i cha-lah. L' - chah do-di
am s'-gu - lah, bo-i cha-lah, bo-i cha-lah. L' - chah do-di,

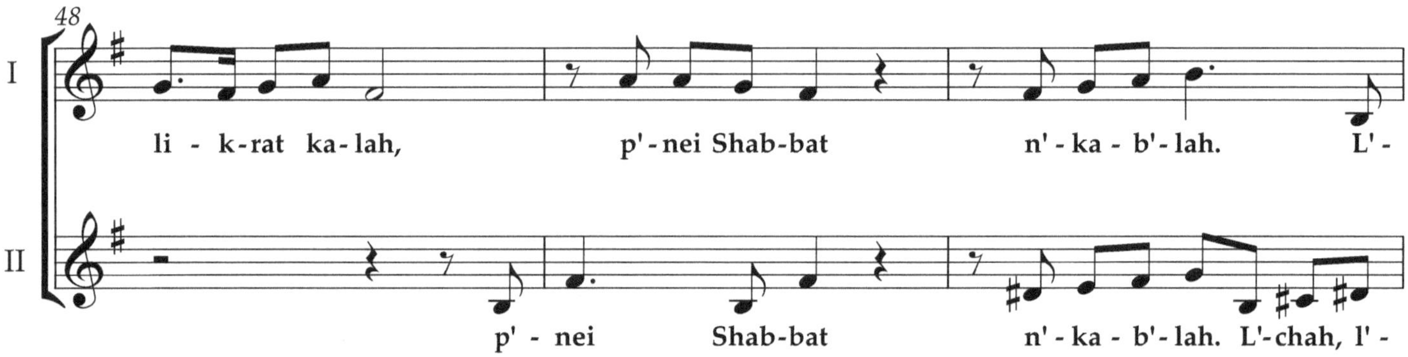
48
I
li - k-rat ka-lah, p'-nei Shab-bat n'-ka - b'-lah. L'-
II
p' - nei Shab-bat n'-ka - b'-lah. L'-chah, l' -

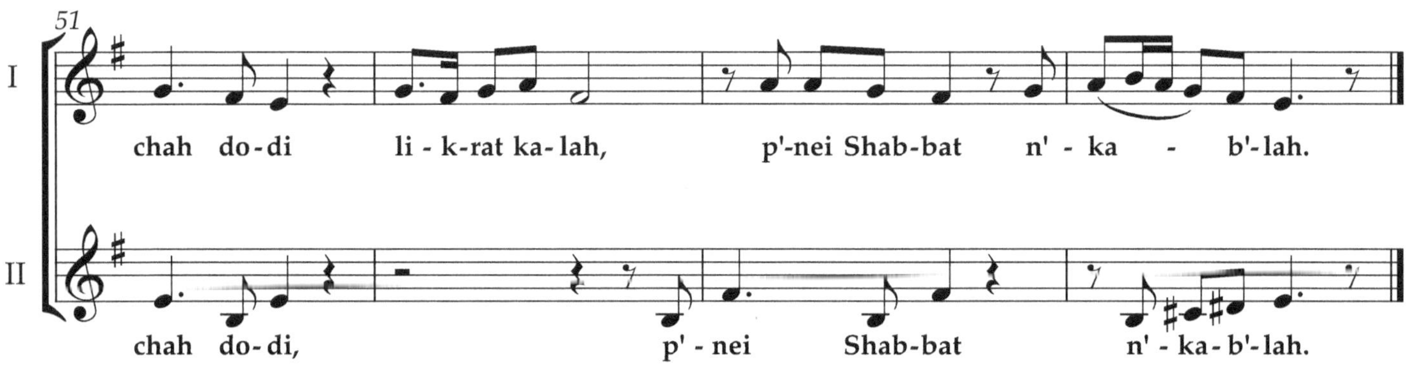
51
I
chah do-di li - k-rat ka-lah, p'-nei Shab-bat n' - ka - b'-lah.
II
chah do-di, p' - nei Shab-bat n' - ka - b'-lah.

Light One Candle

Music and text: **Peter Yarrow**

Arranged by **Susan Lewis Friedman** and **David Berger**
Piano arranged by **Susan Lewis Friedman** and **Gregory Shifrin**
Corresponding band arrangement by **Emily Tummons**

B7 C7 Em Fm Em/D Fm/E♭
mf
right to ex - ist was de - nied. Light one can-dle for the ter - ri - ble sac - ri - fice
right to ex - ist was de - nied. Light one can-dle for the ter - ri - ble sac - ri - fice
C D♭ C/B D♭/C A B♭ G A♭ Em Fm G A♭ Em Fm
jus-tice and free-dom de - mand. Light one can-dle for the wis-dom to know when the
jus-tice and free-dom de - mand. Light one can - dle when the
CHORUS
C D♭ D7 E♭7 G A♭ B7 C7 E7 F7 Am B♭m
peace-mak-er's time is at hand. Don't let the light go out, it's
peace-mak-er's time is at hand. Don't let the light go out, it's

D7 Eb7 G Ab B7 C7 E7 F7 Am Bbm
I
II
last-ed for so ma-ny years. Don't let the light go out, let it
last-ed for so ma-ny years, so ma - ny years. Don't let the light go out, let it
D7 Eb7 G Ab B7 C7 Em Fm
shine through our love and our tears.
shine through our love and our tears.
VERSE 2
G Ab G/F# Ab/G
oo oo oo oo
f melody
Light one can-dle for the strength that we need to nev - er be-come our own

Em Em/D C
Fm Fm/E♭ D♭
melody
I
II
— Light one can - dle for those who are suff' - ring the
foe. oo oo the
B7 Em
C7 Fm
pain we learned so long a - go. Light one can - dle for
pain we learned so long a - go. Light one
Em/D C G/B A G Em
Fm/E♭ D♭ A♭/C B♭ A♭ Fm
all we be-lieve in, that an-ger not tear us a - part. Light one can-dle to
can - dle that an-ger not tear us a - part. Light one

46
G Em C D7 G B7
Ab Fm Db Eb7 Ab C7
I
bind us to - geth - er, with peace as the song in our hearts.
II
can - dle with peace as the song in our hearts.
CHORUS
49
E7 Am D7
F7 Bbm Eb7
I
Don't let the light go out, it's last - ed for so many
II
Don't let the light go out, it's last - ed for so ma - ny
52
G B7 E7 Am
Ab C7 F7 Bbm
I
years. Don't let the light go out, let it
II
years, so ma - ny years. Don't let the light go out, let it

D7 G B Em
E♭7 A♭ C Fm
55
I
shine through our love and our tears.
II
shine through our love and our tears.
VERSE 3
G G/F# Em Em/D
A♭ A♭/G Fm Fm/E♭
59
melody
What is the mem - 'ry that's val-ued so high - ly that we keep a - live in that flame?
What is the mem - 'ry that's val-ued so high - ly that we keep a - live in that flame, that flame?
C B7
D♭ C7
63
melody
What's the com-mit - ment to those who have died that we cry out,"They've not died in vain"?
melody
What's the com-mit - ment to those who have died that we cry out,"They've not died in vain"?

Em Em/D C G/B A
Fm Fm/E♭ D♭ A♭/C B♭
67
melody
I
We have come this__ far____ al-ways be-liev - ing that jus-tice would some-how pre- vail?
melody
II
We have come this__ far al-ways be-liev - ing that jus-tice would some-how pre- vail?
G Em G Em C D7 G B
A♭ Fm A♭ Fm D♭ E♭7 A♭ C
71
This is the bur - den and this is the pro - mise and this is why we will not fail!________
optional descant ("Maoz Tzur")
This is the pro - mise__ and we will not fail!________
CHORUS
E7 Am D7 G B7
F7 B♭m E♭7 A♭ C7
75
Don't let the light go out,__ it's last-ed for so__ ma-ny years.
Don't let the light go out,__ it's last-ed for so__ ma-ny years, so ma - ny__

79
E7 F7 Am B♭m D7 E♭7 G A♭ B7 C7
I
Don't let the light go out, let it shine through our love and our tears.
II
years. Don't let the light go out, let it shine through our love and our tears.
83
E7 F7 Am B♭m E7 F7
I
Don't let the light go out. Don't let the
II
Don't let the light go out. Don't let the
86
Am B♭m E7 F7 Am B♭m
I
light go out. Don't let the light go out!
II
light go out. Don't let the light go out!

Light One Candle

Music and text: **Peter Yarrow**

Arranged by **Susan Lewis Friedman** and **David Berger**
Piano arranged by **Susan Lewis Friedman** and **Gregory Shifrin**
Corresponding band arrangement by **Emily Tummons**

Corresponding band arrangement available in *Kol Han'shamah: Band Volume II* (TMP 994069)

19
I
Light one can-dle for the wis-dom to know_ when the peace-mak-er's time is at
II
Light one can - dle when the peace-mak-er's time is at
22
CHORUS
I
hand._____ Don't let the light go out,_ it's last-ed for so__ ma-ny
II
hand._____ Don't_ let the light go out,_ it's last-ed for so__ ma-ny
26
I
years. Don't let the light go out,__ let it
II
years, so ma - ny years. Don't let the light go out,__ let it
29
I
shine through our love and our tears.__________
II
shine through our love and our tears.__________

VERSE 2
33
I
II
f melody
oo oo oo oo
Light one can-dle for thestrength that we need to nev - er be-come our own
36
melody
Light one can - dle for those who are suff' - ring the
foe. oo oo the
39
pain we learned so long a - go. Light one can - dle for
pain we learned so long a - go. Light one
42
all we be-lieve in, that an-ger not tear us a - part. Light one can-dle to
can - dle that an-ger not tear us a - part. Light one

46
I
bind us to - geth - er, with peace as the song in our hearts.
II
can - dle with peace as the song in our hearts.
CHORUS
49
Don't let the light go out, it's last-ed for so man-y years.
Don't let the light go out, it's last-ed for so man-y years, so man - y
53
Don't let the light go out, let it shine through our love and our
years. Don't let the light go out, let it shine through our love and our
VERSE 3
56
melody
tears. What is the mem - 'ry that's
tears. What is the mem - 'ry that's

60
I
val-ued so high - ly that we keep a - live in that flame?
II
val-ued so high - ly that we keep a - live in that flame, that flame?
63
melody
What's the com-mit - ment to those who have died that we cry out,"They've not died in
melody
What's the com-mit - ment to those who have died that we cry out,"They've not died in
66
vain"?
melody
We have come this far al-ways be - liev - ing that
vain"?
melody
We have come this far al-ways be - liev - ing that
69
jus - tice would some-how pre - vail? This is the bur - den and
optional descant ("Maoz Tzur")
jus - tice would some-how pre - vail? This is the

72
I
this is the pro - mise and this is why we will not fail!
II
pro - mise and we will not fail!
75
CHORUS
I
Don't let the light go out, it's last-ed for so ma-ny
II
Don't let the light go out, it's last-ed for so ma-ny
78
I
years. Don't let the light go out, let it
II
years, so ma - ny years. Don't let the light go out, let it
81
I
shine through our love and our tears. Don't let the
II
shine through our love and our tears. Don't let the
84
I
light go out. Don't let the light go out. Don't let the light go out!
II
light go out. Don't let the light go out. Don't let the light go out!

Mi Chamochah

מי כמוכה

Hebrew text: **Evening liturgy**

Music: **Dan Nichols** and **Mason Cooper**

Arranged by **Susan Lewis Friedman**
Piano arranged by **Susan Lewis Friedman** and **Gregory Shifrin**
Corresponding band arrangement by **Emily Tummons**

Corresponding band arrangement available in *Kol Han'shamah: Band Volume II* (TMP 994069)

C/B
C Eb
Eb/D
A(sus4) C(sus4)
Last time to Coda
A C
B
D F
Em Gm
G Bb
A(sus4) C(sus4)
I
II
desh.
lai.
No - ra,
t' - hi - lot,
Last time to Coda
D F
Em Gm
G Bb
A C
D F
Em Gm
G Bb
A(sus4) C(sus4)
o - seih
No - ra,
fe - le!
t' - hi - lot,
D F
Em Gm
G Bb
A(sus4) C(sus4)
C Eb
Bm Dm
o - seih,
A - do - nai yim - loch l' - o - lam va -
fe - le!
A - do - nai yim - loch l' - o - lam va -

C
melody
I
II
ed. Mal - chu - t'- cha ra - u va - ne - cha, bo-
kei - a yam lif - nei Mo - she u - Mir - yam. Zeh Ei - li, a - nu v'- am' - ru,
zeh Ei - li, a - nu v'- am' - ru, A - do - nai yim - loch l' - o - lam va -
A(sus4) C(sus4) A C D F Em Gm G B♭ A(sus4) C(sus4)
D F Em Gm G B♭ A C
D F Em Gm G B♭ A(sus4) C(sus4) C E♭

CODA

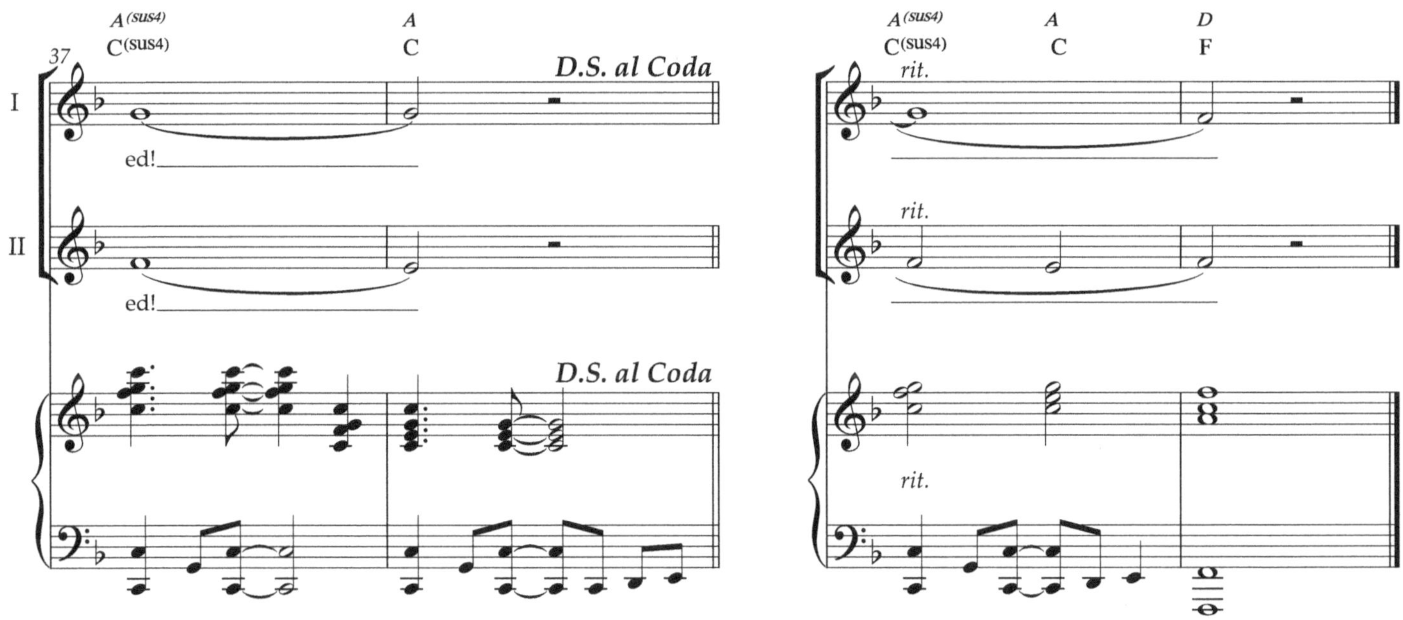

Who is like You, O God, among the gods that are worshiped?
Who is like You, majestic in holiness,
awesome in splendor, working wonders?

מִי־כָמֹכָה בָּאֵלִם, יְיָ!
מִי כָּמֹכָה נֶאְדָּר בַּקֹּדֶשׁ,
נוֹרָא תְהִלֹּת, עֹשֵׂה פֶלֶא!

Your children witnessed Your sovereignty,
the sea splitting before Moses and Miriam.
"This is our God!" they cried.
"Adonai will reign forever and ever!"

מַלְכוּתְךָ רָאוּ בָנֶיךָ,
בּוֹקֵעַ יָם לִפְנֵי מֹשֶׁה וּמִרְיָם.
זֶה אֵלִי, עָנוּ וְאָמְרוּ,
יְיָ יִמְלֹךְ לְעוֹלָם וָעֶד!

Thus it is said, "Adonai redeemed Jacob,
from a hand stronger than his own."
Praised are You, Adonai, for redeeming Israel.

וְנֶאֱמַר: כִּי פָדָה יְיָ אֶת־יַעֲקֹב,
וּגְאָלוֹ מִיַּד חָזָק מִמֶּנּוּ.
בָּרוּךְ אַתָּה, יְיָ, גָּאַל יִשְׂרָאֵל.

Mi Chamochah

מי כמוכה

Hebrew text: **Evening liturgy**

Music: **Dan Nichols** and **Mason Cooper**

Arranged by **Susan Lewis Friedman**
Piano arranged by **Susan Lewis Friedman** and **Gregory Shifrin**
Corresponding band arrangement by **Emily Tummons**

12
I
II
Last time to Coda
B
dar ba - ko - desh.
lai lai lai lai.
No - ra,
t' - hi - lot,
17
o - seih
Nora,
o - seih,
fe - le!
t' - hi - lot,
22
A - do - nai yim - loch l' - o - lam va - ed.
Mal -
fe - le! A - do - nai yim - loch l' - o - lam va - ed.
C
27
chu - t' - cha ra - u va - ne - cha, bo - kei - a yam lif-nei Mo - she u - Mir - yam.

31
melody
I
Zeh Ei - li, a - nu v' - am' - ru, zeh Ei - li, a - nu
II
Zeh Ei - li, a - nu v' - am' - ru, zeh Ei - li, a - nu

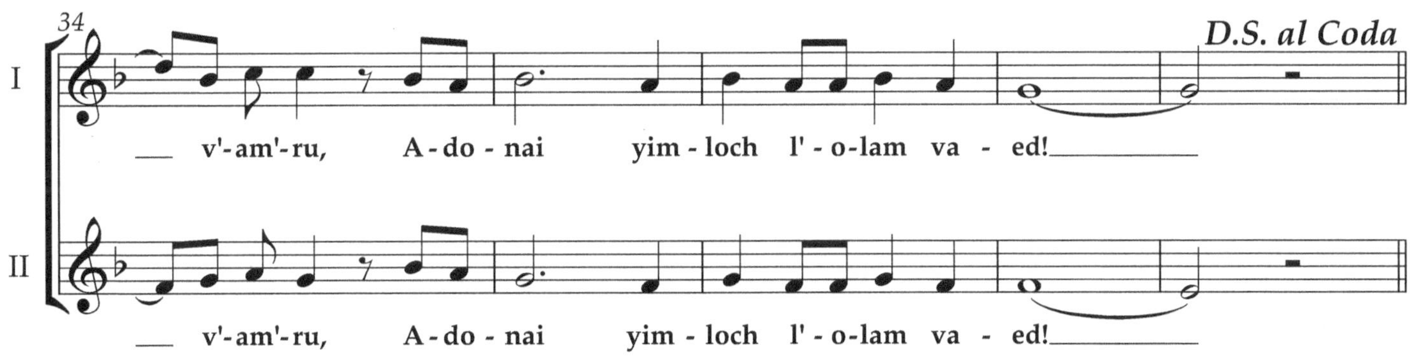
34
D.S. al Coda
I
v'-am'-ru, A - do - nai yim - loch l' - o-lam va - ed!
II
v'-am'-ru, A - do - nai yim - loch l' - o-lam va - ed!

CODA

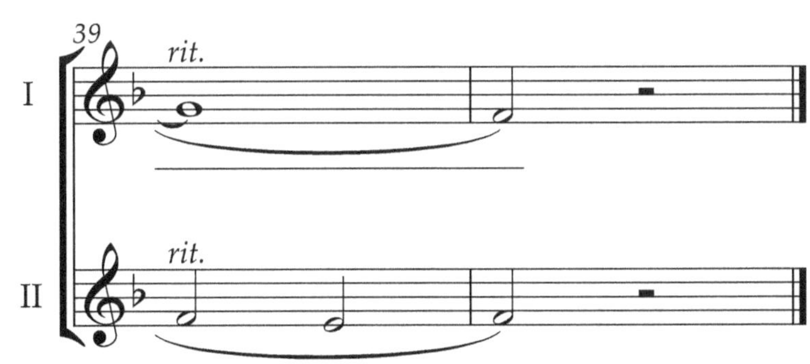
39
rit.
I
rit.
II

Mi Shebeirach

מי שברך

Text: **Debbie Friedman** and **Drorah Setel** (based on liturgy)

Music: **Debbie Friedman**

Arranged by **Susan Lewis Friedman** and **David Berger**
Piano arranged by **Alan Mason**
Corresponding band arrangement by **Emily Tummons**

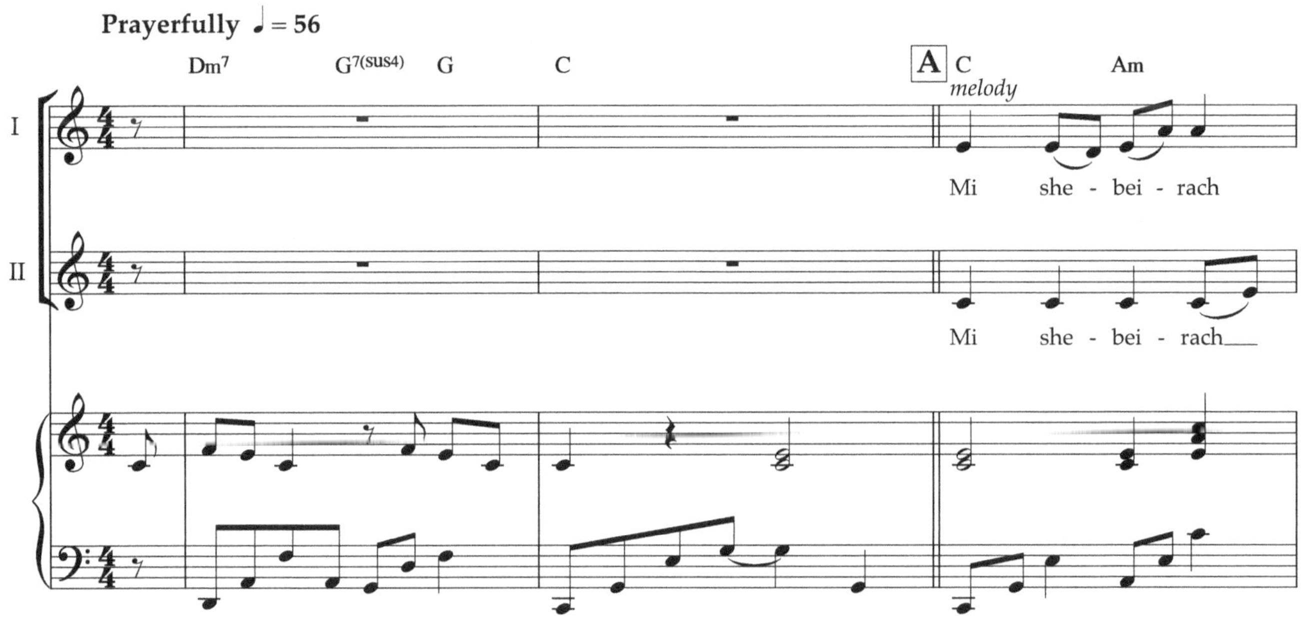

7
Am Em F G C Dm7 Em
I
May the Source of strength who blessed the ones be - fore us help us find the cour-age to
II
May the Source of strength who blessed the ones be - fore us help us find cour-age
10
Dm Am7 Dm7 G7 C
make our lives a bless-ing, and let us say, a - mein.
a bless - ing and let us say, a - mein.
B
13
C Am Em F G(sus4) G C Am
Mi she - bei - rach i - mo - tei - nu m' - kor ha - b'ra - chah la -
melody
Mi she - bei - rach i - mo - tei - nu m' - kor ha - b'ra - chah la -

May the One who blessed our fathers
be the source of blessing for our mothers.
May the One who blessed our mothers
be the source of blessing for our fathers.

מִי שֶׁבֵּרַךְ אֲבוֹתֵינוּ
מְקוֹר הַבְּרָכָה לְאִמּוֹתֵינוּ.
מִי שֶׁבֵּרַךְ אִמּוֹתֵינוּ
מְקוֹר הַבְּרָכָה לַאֲבוֹתֵינוּ.

Mi Shebeirach

מי שברך

Text: **Debbie Friedman** and **Drorah Setel** (based on liturgy)

Music: **Debbie Friedman**

Arranged by **Susan Lewis Friedman** and **David Berger**
Piano arranged by **Alan Mason**
Corresponding band arrangement by **Emily Tummons**

Corresponding band arrangement available in *Kol Han'shamah: Band Volume II* (TMP 994069)

11
B
I
let us say, a - mein.
Mi she - bei - rach
II
melody
let us___ say, a - mein.
Mi she - bei - rach
14
I
melody
i - mo - tei - nu m'-kor ha-b'ra-chah___ la - a - vo - tei - nu. Bless
II
i - mo - tei - nu m'-kor ha-b'ra-chah___ la - a - vo - tei - nu. Bless
17
I
those in need of heal-ing with r' - fu - ah sh'lei-mah, the re-new-al of bo-dy, the re-
II
melody
those in need of heal-ing with r' - fu - ah sh'lei-mah, the re-new-al of bo-dy, the re-
20
I
new-al of spir-it,___ and let us say, a - mein, a - mein,___
II
new-al of spir-it, and let us say,___ a - mein, a -
23
I
a - mein, a - mein.___
II
mein,___ a - mein.___

Olam Chesed Yibaneh

עולם חסד יבנה

Hebrew text: **Psalm 89:3**

Music and English text: **Menachem Creditor**

Arranged by **Rachelle Nelson**
Corresponding band arrangement by **Emily Tummons**

Corresponding band arrangement available in *Kol Han'shamah: Band Volume II* (TMP 994069)

13
Cmaj7 D(add9) Em
D♭maj7 E♭(add9) Fm
B
Em D(add9) C D
Fm E♭(add9) D♭ E♭
I
O - lam che-sed yi-ba - neh, ya la lai lai lai lai
II
18
Em D(add9) C D Em
Fm E♭(add9) D♭ E♭ Fm
lai. O - lam che-sed yi-ba - neh, ya la lai lai lai lai lai.
O - lam che-sed yi-ba - neh, ya la lai lai lai lai lai.
23
C
G D(add9) C D Em G
A♭ E♭(add9) D♭ E♭ Fm A♭
O - lam che-sed yi-ba - neh, ya la lai lai lai lai lai. O - lam che-sed yi-ba-
O - lam che-sed yi-ba-

28
D(add9) Eb(add9) D Eb C Db D Eb Em Fm
D Em Fm
I
neh, ya la lai lai lai lai lai lai.
I will build this world from
II
neh, ya la lai lai lai lai lai lai.
32
D(add9) Eb(add9) C Db D Eb Em Fm
I
love, ya la lai lai lai lai lai, and you must build this world from
II
ya la lai lai lai lai lai
36
D(add9) Eb(add9) C Db D Eb Em Fm
E G Ab
I
love, ya la lai lai lai lai lai. And if we build this world from
II
ya la lai lai lai lai lai.

D(add9) Eb(add9) C Db D Eb Em Fm G Ab
love, ya la lai lai lai lai__ lai, then God will build this world from
ya la lai lai lai lai__ lai
D(add9) Eb(add9) C Db D Eb Em Fm F Em Fm
love, ya la lai lai lai lai__ lai lai. oo
ya la lai lai lai lai__ lai lai oo
D(add9) Eb(add9) Cmaj7 Dbmaj7 D(add9) Eb(add9) Em Fm
oo oo
oo oo

Your steadfast love is confirmed forever. עוֹלָם חֶסֶד יִבָּנֶה.

Olam Chesed Yibaneh

עולם חסד יבנה

Hebrew text: **Psalm 89:3**

Music and English text: **Menachem Creditor**

Arranged by **Rachelle Nelson**
Corresponding band arrangement by **Emily Tummons**

Corresponding band arrangement available in *Kol Han'shamah: Band Volume II* (TMP 994069)

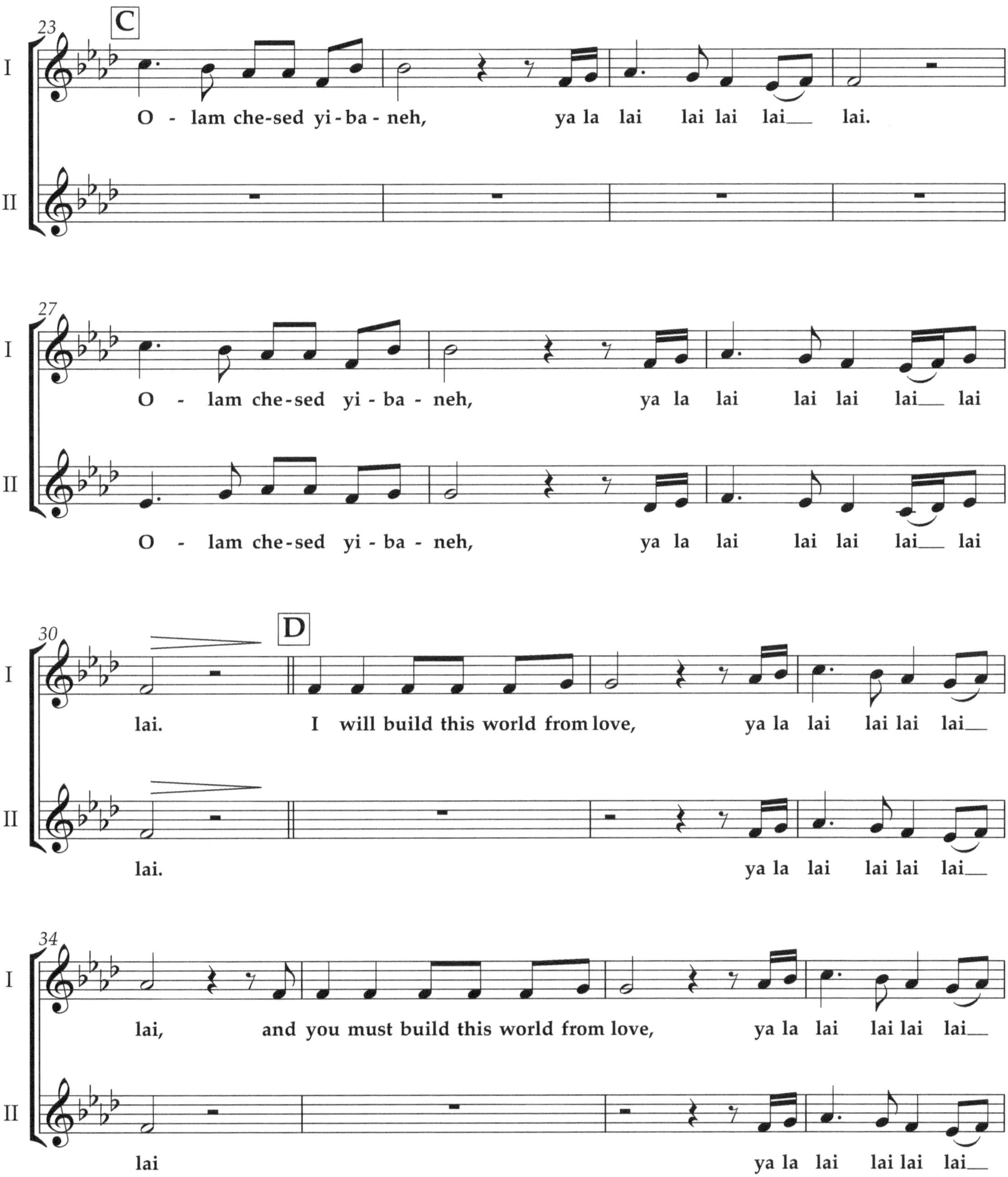
C
O - lam che-sed yi-ba - neh, ya la lai lai lai lai__ lai.
O - lam che-sed yi - ba - neh, ya la lai lai lai lai__ lai
O - lam che-sed yi - ba - neh, ya la lai lai lai lai__ lai
D
lai. I will build this world from love, ya la lai lai lai lai__
lai. ya la lai lai lai lai__
lai, and you must build this world from love, ya la lai lai lai lai__
lai ya la lai lai lai lai__

E
I
II
lai. And if we build this world from love, ya la lai lai lai lai
lai. ya la lai lai lai lai
lai, then God will build this world from love, ya la lai lai lai lai lai
lai ya la lai lai lai lai lai
F
lai. oo oo
lai oo oo
oo ya la lai lai lai lai lai lai.
rit.
oo ya la lai lai lai lai lai lai.

Oseh Shalom עושה שלום

Hebrew text: **Liturgy**

Music and English text: **Elana Jagoda**

Arranged by **Susan Lewis Friedman**
Piano arranged by **Susan Lewis Friedman** and **Gregory Shifrin**
Corresponding band arrangement by **Emily Tummons**

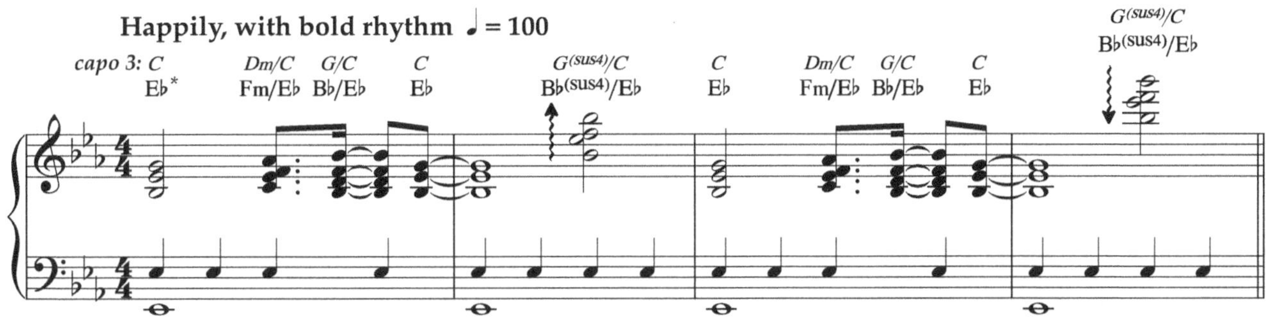

* Guitarists may play standard chord forms

Corresponding band arrangement available in *Kol Han'shamah: Band Volume II* (TMP 994069)

C C/B Am F(add9)
E♭ E♭/D B Cm A♭(add9)
12
I
hu ya - a - seh, hu ya - a - seh, hu ya - a - seh
II
hu ya - a - seh
C G Am F(add9)
E♭ B♭ Cm A♭(add9)
14
shalom, hu ya - a - seh, hu ya - a - seh, hu ya - a - seh
melody
sha - lom, hu ya - a - seh, hu ya - a - seh, hu ya - a - seh
C G Am F(add9)
E♭ B♭ Cm A♭(add9)
16
melody
sha - lom, hu ya - a - seh, hu ya - a - seh, hu ya - a - seh
sha - lom, hu ya - a - seh, hu ya - a - seh

C Eb G Bb G(add9) Bb(add9)
I
sha-lom a - lei - nu.
II
sha-lom a - lei - nu.
8va
C
Fmaj7 Ab maj7 G Bb Am Cm F(add9) Ab(add9)
1. D.S.
2. Continue
May the One, may the One who makes peace bring peace down, bring peace down.
May the One, may the One who makes peace bring peace down, bring peace down.
1. D.S.
2. Continue
D
optional
Solo
O - - - seh sha - lom,
May the One, may the One who makes peace bring peace down, bring peace down.
May the One, may the One who makes peace bring peace down, bring peace down.

May the One who makes peace in the high heavens
make peace for us.

עֹשֶׂה שָׁלוֹם בִּמְרוֹמָיו,
הוּא יַעֲשֶׂה שָׁלוֹם עָלֵינוּ.

Oseh Shalom

עושה שלום

Hebrew text: **Liturgy**

Music and English text: **Elana Jagoda**

Arranged by **Susan Lewis Friedman**
Piano arranged by **Susan Lewis Friedman** and **Gregory Shifrin**
Corresponding band arrangement by **Emily Tummons**

Corresponding band arrangement available in *Kol Han'shamah: Band Volume II* (TMP 994069)

13
B
I
hu ya-a-seh, hu ya-a-seh sha-lom, hu ya-a-seh,
II
melody
hu ya - a - seh sha-lom, hu ya-a-seh,
15
I
hu ya-a-seh, hu ya-a-seh sha-lom, hu ya-a-seh,
II
hu ya-a-seh, hu ya-a-seh sha-lom, hu ya-a-seh,
17
melody
I
hu ya-a-seh, hu ya-a-seh sha-lom a - lei - nu.
II
hu ya - a - seh sha-lom a - lei - nu.
21
C
1. D.S.
2. Continue
I
May the One, may the One who makes peace bring peace down, bring peace down.
II
May the One, may the One who makes peace bring peace down, bring peace down.

23
D
optional
Solo
O - - seh sha - lom,
I
May the One, may the One who makes peace bring peace down, bring peace down.
II
May the One, may the One who makes peace bring peace down, bring peace down.
25
Repeat as desired
ad lib.
o - - seh sha - lom.
May the One, may the One who makes peace bring peace down, bring peace down.
May the One, may the One who makes peace bring peace down, bring peace down.
27
End
rit.
hu ya - a - seh sha - lom a - lei - nu.
peace down, bring peace down. a - lei - nu.
peace down, bring peace down. a - lei - nu.

Shalom Aleichem

שלום עליכם

Text: **Liturgy**

Music: **Sol Zim**

Arranged by **Robbie Solomon**
Corresponding band arrangement by **Emily Tummons**

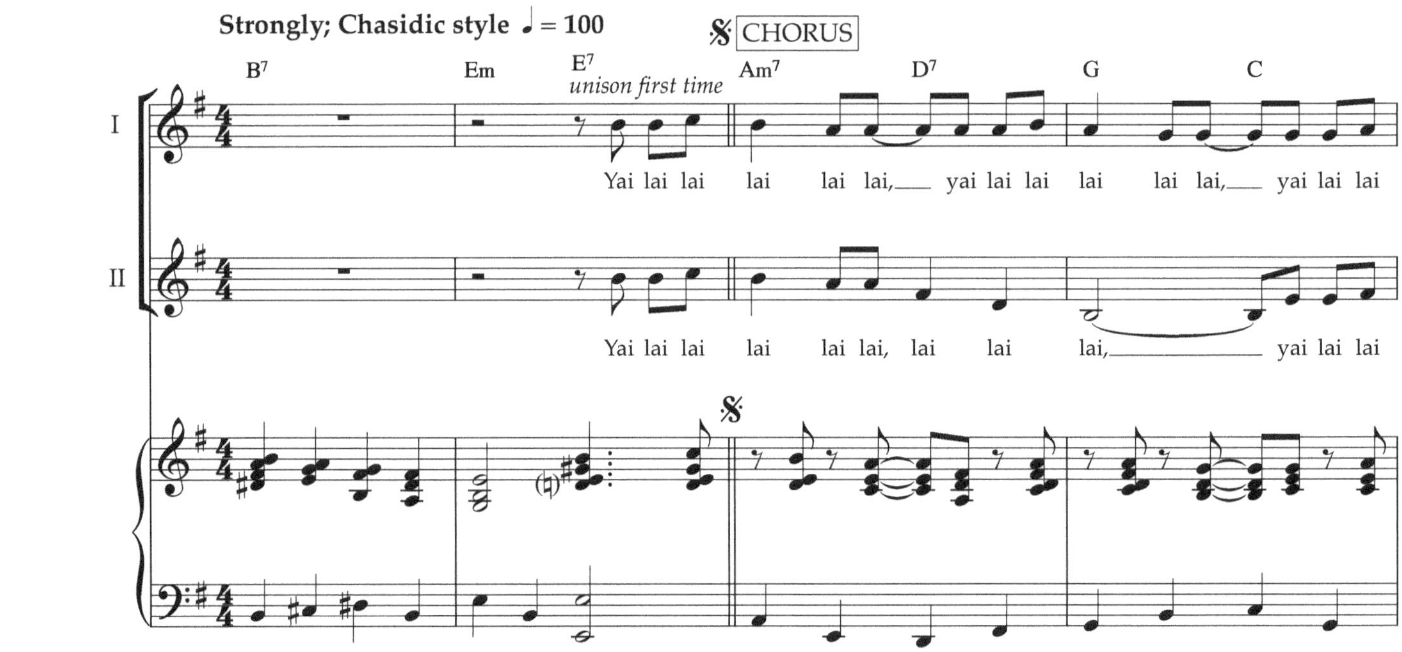

Corresponding band arrangement available in *Kol Han'shamah: Band Volume II* (TMP 994069)

VERSES
Am7 B7 Em B7 Em
I
lai lai lai, lai lai lai lai. 1. Sha - lom a - lei - chem, mal - a - chei ha - sha - reit,
2. Bar' - chu - ni l'-sha - lom, mal - a - chei ha - sha - lom,
II
lai lai lai, lai lai lai lai. 1. a - lei - chem ha - sha - reit,
2. l' - sha - lom ha - sha - lom,
Am6 B7
mal - a - chei el - yon, mi - me - lech, mi me - lech mal - chei ham'-la - chim, Ha-
mal - a - chei el - yon, mi - me - lech, mi me - lech mal - chei ham'-la - chim, Ha-
el - yon, mi - me - lech, ham'-la - chim,
el - yon, mi - me - lech, ham'-la - chim,
Cmaj7 D7(sus4) D7 G B7 Em
Ka - dosh, ba - ruch hu. Bo - a - chem l'-sha - lom, mal - a - chei ha - sha - lom,
Ka - dosh, ba - ruch hu. Tzeit - chem l'-sha - lom, mal - a - chei ha - sha - lom,
Ka - dosh, ba - ruch hu. l'-sha - lom, ha - sha - lom,
Ka - dosh, ba - ruch hu. l'-sha - lom, ha - sha - lom,

21
Am6 B7
I
mal - a - chei el - yon, mi - me - lech, mi - me - lech
mal - a - chei el - yon, mi - me - lech, mi me - lech
II
el - yon, mi - me - lech,
el - yon, mi - me - lech,
24
Em E7
1. D.S.
2. D.S. al Coda
mal-chei ham'-la-chim, Ha - Ka - dosh, ba - ruch hu.
Yai lai lai
mal-chei ham'-la-chim, Ha - Ka - dosh, ba - ruch hu.
ham'-la-chim. Ka - dosh, ba - ruch hu.
Yai lai lai
ham'-la-chim. Ka - dosh, ba - ruch hu.
1. D.S.
2. D.S. al Coda
CODA
27
Am7 B7 Em B7 Em
non-rit.
lai lai lai, lai lai lai lai.
non-rit.
lai lai lai, lai lai lai lai.
non-rit.

Peace be to you, O ministering angels,
messengers of the Most High,
Majesty of majesties,
Holy One of Blessing.

שָׁלוֹם עֲלֵיכֶם, מַלְאֲכֵי הַשָּׁרֵת,
מַלְאֲכֵי עֶלְיוֹן,
מִמֶּלֶךְ מַלְכֵי הַמְּלָכִים,
הַקָּדוֹשׁ בָּרוּךְ הוּא.

Enter in peace, O messengers of peace,
angels of the Most High,
Majesty of majesties,
Holy One of Blessing.

בּוֹאֲכֶם לְשָׁלוֹם, מַלְאֲכֵי הַשָּׁלוֹם,
מַלְאֲכֵי עֶלְיוֹן,
מִמֶּלֶךְ מַלְכֵי הַמְּלָכִים,
הַקָּדוֹשׁ בָּרוּךְ הוּא.

Bless me with peace, O messengers of peace,
angels of the Most High,
Majesty of majesties,
Holy One of Blessing.

בָּרְכוּנִי לְשָׁלוֹם, מַלְאֲכֵי הַשָּׁלוֹם,
מַלְאֲכֵי עֶלְיוֹן,
מִמֶּלֶךְ מַלְכֵי הַמְּלָכִים,
הַקָּדוֹשׁ בָּרוּךְ הוּא.

Depart in peace, O messengers of peace,
angels of the Most High,
Majesty of majesties,
Holy One of Blessing.

צֵאתְכֶם לְשָׁלוֹם, מַלְאֲכֵי הַשָּׁלוֹם,
מַלְאֲכֵי עֶלְיוֹן,
מִמֶּלֶךְ מַלְכֵי הַמְּלָכִים,
הַקָּדוֹשׁ בָּרוּךְ הוּא.

Shalom Aleichem

שלום עליכם

Text: **Liturgy**

Music: **Sol Zim**

Arranged by **Robbie Solomon**
Corresponding band arrangement by **Emily Tummons**

12
I
mal-a-chei ha-sha-reit, mal-a-chei el - yon, mi -
mal-a-chei ha-sha-lom, mal-a-chei el - yon, mi -
II
ha-sha-reit, el - yon,
ha-sha-lom, el - yon,
15
I
me-lech, mi me-lech mal-chei ham'-la-chim, Ha - Ka - dosh, ba - ruch
me-lech, mi me-lech mal-chei ham'-la-chim, Ha - Ka - dosh, ba - ruch
II
mi-me-lech, ham'-la-chim, Ka - dosh, ba - ruch
mi-me-lech, ham'-la-chim, Ka - dosh, ba - ruch
18
I
hu. Bo-a-chem l' - sha-lom, mal-a-chei ha-sha-lom,
hu. Tzeit-chem l' - sha-lom, mal-a-chei ha-sha-lom,
II
hu. l' - sha-lom, ha-sha-lom,
hu. l' - sha-lom, ha-sha-lom,
21
I
mal-a-chei el - yon, mi - me-lech, mi-me-lech
mal-a-chei el - yon, mi - me-lech, mi me-lech
II
el - yon, mi-me-lech,
el - yon, mi-me-lech,

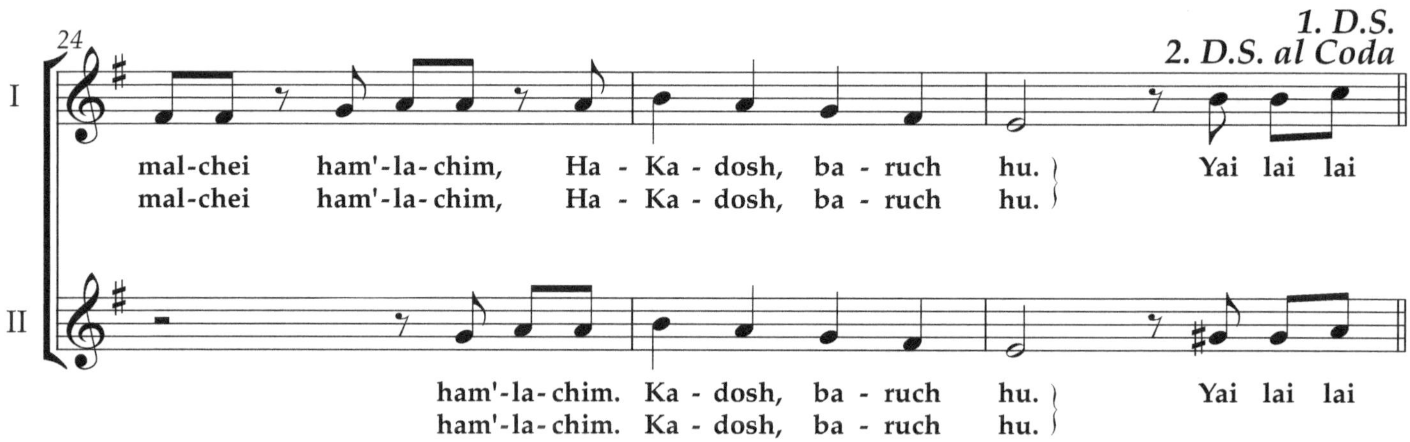
24
1. D.S.
2. D.S. al Coda
I
mal-chei ham'-la-chim, Ha - Ka - dosh, ba - ruch hu. Yai lai lai
mal-chei ham'-la-chim, Ha - Ka - dosh, ba - ruch hu.
II
ham'-la-chim. Ka - dosh, ba - ruch hu. Yai lai lai
ham'-la-chim. Ka - dosh, ba - ruch hu.

CODA

27
non-rit.
I
lai lai lai,__ lai lai lai lai.
non-rit.
II
lai lai lai,__ lai lai lai lai.

Shalom Rav

שלום רב

Text: **Evening liturgy**

Music: **Jeff Klepper** and **Dan Freelander**

Arranged by **Rachelle Nelson**
Piano arranged by **Rachelle Nelson** and **Gregory Shifrin**
Corresponding band arrangement by **Emily Tummons**

* *For introduction and A, C, and E sections, guitarists may play standard chord forms*

Corresponding band arrangement available in *Kol Han'shamah: Band Volume II* (TMP 994069)

13
D(add9) C(add9)/D G/D A/D D
I
rav al Yis-ra - el am' - cha ta - sim l' - o - lam.
II
rav al Yis-ra - el am' - cha ta - sim l' - o - lam.
17
B
A G(add9) A(sus4) A G
Ki a-tah hu Me-lech A-don l'-chol ha - sha - lom,
Ki a-tah hu Me-lech A-don l'-chol ha - sha - lom,
21
A G(add9) Em7 A(sus4) A
ki a-tah hu Me-lech A-don l'-chol ha - sha - lom. Sha-lom
ki a-tah hu Me-lech A-don l'-chol ha - sha - lom. Sha-lom

25
C D(add9) C(add9)/D G/D A/D
I
rav al Yis-ra - el am' - cha ta - sim l' - o - lam, sha-lom
II
rav al Yis-ra - el am' - cha ta - sim l' - o - lam, sha-lom
optional
III
oo
29
D(add9) C(add9)/D G/D A/D D
I
rav al Yis-ra - el am' - cha ta - sim l' - o - lam. V'-
tutti
II
rav al Yis-ra - el am' - cha ta - sim l' - o - lam. V'-
III
oo

33
D
Em C D D/C♯ Bm Bm/A Em A(sus4) A D F♯7(sus4) F♯7
I
tov b'-ei-ne-cha l'-va-reich et am'-cha Yis-ra-el
II
tov b'-ei-ne-cha l'-va-reich et am'-cha Yis-ra-el
37
Em F♯7 Bm Bm/A Em G/A G A
I
b'-chol eit u-v-chol sha-ah bish-lo-me-cha. Sha-lom
II
b'-chol eit u-v-chol sha-ah bish-lo-me-cha. Sha-lom

41
E
D(add9) C(add9)/D G/D A/D
I
rav al Yis-ra-el am'-cha ta-sim l'-o-lam, sha-lom
II
rav al Yis-ra-el am'-cha ta-sim l'-o-lam, sha-lom
optional
III
oo
45
D(add9) C(add9)/D G/D A/D D
I
rav al Yis-ra-el am'-cha ta-sim l'-o-lam, ta-
tutti
II
rav al Yis-ra-el am'-cha ta-sim l'-o-lam, ta-
III
oo

Grant abundant peace to Israel
Your people forever,
for You are the Sovereign God
of all peace.
May it be pleasing to You
to bless Your people Israel
in every season and moment with Your peace.

שָׁלוֹם רָב עַל יִשְׂרָאֵל עַמְּךָ
תָּשִׂים לְעוֹלָם,
כִּי אַתָּה הוּא מֶלֶךְ אָדוֹן
לְכָל הַשָּׁלוֹם.
וְטוֹב בְּעֵינֶיךָ לְבָרֵךְ
אֶת עַמְּךָ יִשְׂרָאֵל
בְּכָל עֵת וּבְכָל שָׁעָה בִּשְׁלוֹמֶךָ.

Shalom Rav

שלום רב

Text: **Evening liturgy**

Music: **Jeff Klepper** and **Dan Freelander**

Arranged by **Rachelle Nelson**
Piano arranged by **Rachelle Nelson** and **Gregory Shifrin**
Corresponding band arrangement by **Emily Tummons**

Corresponding band arrangement available in *Kol Han'shamah: Band Volume II* (TMP 994069)

17
B
I
Ki a-tah hu Me-lech A-don l'-chol ha - sha - lom,
II
Ki a-tah hu Me-lech A-don l'-chol ha - sha - lom,
21
I
ki a-tah hu Me-lech A-don l'-chol ha - sha - lom. Sha-lom
II
ki a-tah hu Me-lech A-don l'-chol ha - sha - lom. Sha-lom
25
C
I
rav al Yis-ra - el am'-cha ta - sim l' - o - lam, sha-lom
II
rav al Yis-ra - el am'-cha ta - sim l' - o - lam, sha-lom
optional
III
oo

29
I
rav al Yis-ra - el am'-cha ta - sim l'-o - lam. V'-
II
tutti
rav al Yis-ra - el am'-cha ta - sim l'-o - lam. V'-
III
oo
D
33
I
tov b'-ei-ne-cha l'-va-reich et am-cha Yis-ra-el
II
tov b'-ei-ne-cha l'-va-reich et am-cha Yis-ra-el
37
I
b'-chol eit u-v-chol sha-ah bish-lo-me - cha. Sha-lom
II
b'-chol eit u-v-chol sha-ah bish-lo-me - cha. Sha-lom

E
41
I
rav al Yis-ra - el am'-cha ta - sim l' - o - lam, sha-lom
II
rav al Yis-ra - el am'-cha ta - sim l' - o - lam, sha-lom
optional
III
oo
45
I
rav al Yis-ra - el am' - cha ta - sim l' - o - lam, ta-
tutti
II
rav al Yis-ra - el am' - cha ta - sim l' - o - lam, ta-
III
oo
49
rit.
I
sim l' - o - lam, ta - sim l' - o - lam.
rit.
II
sim l' - o - lam, ta - sim l' - o - lam.

Shir Chadash

שיר חדש

Hebrew text: **Based on Psalm 96:1**

Music and English text: **Julie Silver**

Arranged by **Robbie Solomon**
Corresponding band arrangement by **Emily Tummons**

* *Optional Part III: This is the harmony part originally composed by Julie Silver. It can be sung instead of Part II or as an added part.*

Corresponding band arrangement available in *Kol Han'shamah: Band Volume II* (TMP 994069)

17
Dm7 G Last time to Coda 1. C(sus4) G 2. C(sus4) C
I
shir cha - dash. dash.
II
shir cha - dash. dash.
III
nai.
Last time to Coda
B
23
Bb F C(sus4) C Bb F
I
Sing un - to God, all the earth, a new song. I will sing un - to God a new
tutti
II
Sing un - to God, all the earth, a new song. I will sing un - to God a new

29
C
B♭
F
C(sus4) C
I
song.
Sing un - to God and we'll all sing a-long, all the
II
song.
Sing un - to God and we'll all sing a-long, all the
35
B♭
F
G7(sus4)
G7
Dm7
G7
D.S. al Coda
I
earth, a new song, un - to God.
optional divisi
II
earth, a new song, un - to God.
D.S. al Coda

CODA

Sing unto God a new song,
sing unto God, all the earth.

שִׁירוּ לַיָי כָּל הָאָרֶץ,
שִׁירוּ לַיָי שִׁיר חָדָשׁ.

Shir Chadash

שיר חדש

Hebrew text: **Based on Psalm 96:1**

Music and English text: **Julie Silver**

Arranged by **Robbie Solomon**
Corresponding band arrangement by **Emily Tummons**

** Optional Part III: This is the harmony part originally composed by Julie Silver. It can be sung instead of Part II or as an added part.*

Corresponding band arrangement available in *Kol Han'shamah: Band Volume II* (TMP 994069)

Last time to Coda
1.
2.
17
I
shir cha - dash. dash.
II
shir cha - dash. dash.
III
nai.
B
23
I
Sing un - to God, all the earth, a new song. I will sing un - to
tutti
II
Sing un - to God, all the earth, a new song. I will sing un - to
28
I
God a new song. Sing un - to God and we'll all sing a-long,
II
God a new song. Sing un - to God and we'll all sing a-long,

34
D.S. al Coda
I
all the earth, a new song, un - to God.
optional divisi
II
all the earth, a new song, un - to God.

CODA

41
molto rit.
I
dash. I will sing un - to God a new song.
II
dash. I will sing un - to God a new song.
III
I will sing un - to God a new song.

Y'did Nefesh

ידיד נפש

Text: **Eleazar ben Moses Azikri**

Music: **Ehud** and **Sarah Zweig**

Arranged by **Robbie Solomon**
Corresponding band arrangement by **Emily Tummons**

Corresponding band arrangement available in *Kol Han'shamah: Band Volume II* (TMP 994069)

25
Am B7 Em Em7 Am B7 Em E7/G#
I
m' - shoch av - d' - cha d' di di dai dai dai el r' - tzo - ne - cha.
II
m' - shoch av - d' - cha el r' - tzo - ne - cha.
33
B
Am D7 G Cmaj7 Am D7 G Em
Ya - rutz av - d' - cha k' - mo a - yal
Ya - rutz av - d' - cha k' - mo a - yal
41
A/C# B7/D# Em Em7/D Am B7
yish - ta - cha - veh ai d' di di dai dai dai el mul ha - da - re -
yish - ta - cha - veh ai dai el mul ha - da - re -

47
Em E7/G♯ C Am D7 G Cmaj7 Am
poco a poco accel.
I
cha. Ya - rutz av - d' - cha k' -
II
cha. Ya - rutz av - d' - cha k' -
54
D7 G E7 Am B7 Cmaj7
mo a - yal yish - ta - cha - veh ai d' di di
mo a - yal yish - ta - cha - veh ai
60
Em7 Am B7 Em
molto rit.
dai dai dai el mul ha - da - re - cha.
dai el mul ha - da - re - cha.

Heart's delight, Source of mercy,
draw Your servant into Your arms.
I leap like a deer
to stand in awe before You.

יְדִיד נֶפֶשׁ, אָב הָרַחֲמָן,
מְשׁוֹךְ עַבְדְּךָ אֶל רְצוֹנֶךָ.
יָרוּץ עַבְדְּךָ כְּמוֹ אַיָּל
יִשְׁתַּחֲוֶה אֶל מוּל הֲדָרֶךָ.

Y'did Nefesh

ידיד נפש

Text: **Eleazar ben Moses Azikri**

Music: **Ehud** and **Sarah Zweig**

Arranged by **Robbie Solomon**
Corresponding band arrangement by **Emily Tummons**

Corresponding band arrangement available in *Kol Han'shamah: Band Volume II* (TMP 994069)

36
I
cha k' - mo a - yal yish-ta-cha - veh ai d' di di
II
cha k' - mo a - yal yish-ta-cha - veh ai
44
C
poco a poco accel.
dai dai dai el mul ha - da - re - cha. Ya - rutz
poco a poco accel.
dai el mul ha - da - re - cha. Ya - rutz
51
av - d' - cha k' - mo a - yal yish - ta - cha -
av - d' - cha k' - mo a - yal yish - ta - cha -
58
molto rit.
veh ai d' di di dai dai dai el mul ha - da - re - cha.
molto rit.
veh ai dai el mul ha - da - re - cha.

Yih'yu L'ratzon

יהיו לרצון

Text: **Liturgy**

Music: **Hollis Schachner**

Arranged by **Rachelle Nelson**
Corresponding band arrangement by **Emily Tummons**

Corresponding band arrangement available in *Kol Han'shamah: Band Volume II* (TMP 994069)

F G C(add9) G/B Last time to Coda Am F
I
II
A-do-nai, tzu-ri v'-go-a-li, A-do-
A-do-nai, tzu-ri v'-go-a-li, A-do-
Last time to Coda
C B♭ G C G/B mf B Am
nai, tzu-ri v'-go-a-li. May the words of
nai, tzu-ri v'-go-a-li. May the words of
mf
mf
Em F C F C G/B Am Em
my mouth and the med-i-ta-tions of my
my mouth and the med-i-ta-tions of my

May the words of my mouth and the meditations of my heart be acceptable to You, Adonai, my Rock and my Redeemer.

יִהְיוּ לְרָצוֹן אִמְרֵי פִי וְהֶגְיוֹן לִבִּי
לְפָנֶיךָ, יְיָ, צוּרִי וְגוֹאֲלִי.

Yih'yu L'ratzon

יהיו לרצון

Text: **Liturgy**

Music: **Hollis Schachner**

Arranged by **Rachelle Nelson**
Corresponding band arrangement by **Emily Tummons**

Corresponding band arrangement available in *Kol Han'shamah: Band Volume II* (TMP 994069)

B
mf
D.S. al Coda
mp
nai, tzu - ri v'-go - a - li.
May the words of
my mouth and the med - i - ta - tions of my
and the med - i - ta - tions of my
heart be ac-cept - a-ble to You, A-do - nai,
my Rock and my Re-deem - er. Yi- h'-
my Rock, my Rock my Re - deem- er.

CODA

35
I
mp
rit.
go - a - li, A - do - nai, tzu - ri v' - go - a -
II
mp
rit.
go - a - li, A - do - nai, tzu - ri v' - go - a -
39
I
li.
II
li.

Yism'chu

ישמחו

Text: **Shabbat Liturgy**

Music: **Traditional Chasidic**

Arranged by **Robbie Solomon**
Corresponding band arrangement by **Emily Tummons**

Corresponding band arrangement available in *Kol Han'shamah: Band Volume II* (TMP 994069)

F E Dm7 E F E Dm7 Dm F/C Bm7(b5) E
optional divisi
I
shom - rei, shom - rei, shom - rei Shab - bat v'- ko - rei o - neg, Shab - bat.
II
shom - rei, shom - rei, shom - rei Shab - bat v'- ko - rei o - neg, Shab - bat.
Rubato ♩ = ca. 92
B E7 Am F B°/D E
1. ah m'-ka - d'-shei, Shab - bat,
2. ah ra - tzi - ta - bo, Shab - bat,
3. ah l'- ma - a - seih, Shab - bat,
1. Am m' - ka - d'-shei m' - ka - d'-shei sh'- vi - i, Shab - bat, ku-
(2.) i ra - tzi - ta bo, ra - tzi - ta bo v'- ki - dash - to, Shab - bat, chem-
3. Zei - cher l' - ma - a - seih, l' - ma - a - seih v'- rei - shit, Shab - bat,
Am Last time to Coda Dm/F Bm7(b5) Tempo I E Bm7(b5)
tutti
ah, yis - b'- u, Shab - bat.
ah, ya - mim, Shab - bat.
ah, l'- ma - a - seih,
lam yis - b' - u v' - yit - an - gu mi - tu - ve - cha, Shab - bat.
dat ya - mim o - to ka - ra - ta, Shab - bat.
zei - cher l' - ma - a - seih l' -
Last time to Coda

C
E F E Dm7 E F E Dm7
I
Yis - m' - chu v' - ma - l - chu - t' - cha shom - rei, shom - rei, shom - rei Shab - bat v'-
II
Yis - m' - chu v' - ma - l - chu - t' - cha shom - rei, shom - rei, shom - rei Shab - bat v'-
Dm F/C Bm7(b5) 1. E 2. E
D.S.
D.S. al Coda
ko - rei o - neg Shab - bat. Shab - bat.
ko - rei o - neg Shab - bat. 2. V'-hash- vi - Shab - bat.
CODA
Tempo I
Dm/F Bm7(b5) E Bm7(b5)
D
E
Sha - bat. Yis - m' - chu v' - ma - l - chu - t' - cha
ma - a - seih v' - rei - shit, Sha - bat. Yis - m' - chu v' - ma - l - chu - t' - cha

Those who keep Shabbat
by calling it a delight will rejoice in Your realm.
The people that hallow Shabbat
will delight in Your goodness.
For, being pleased with the Seventh Day,
You hallowed it as the most precious of days,
drawing our attention to the work of Creation.

יִשְׂמְחוּ בְמַלְכוּתְךָ
שׁוֹמְרֵי שַׁבָּת וְקוֹרְאֵי עֹנֶג.
עַם מְקַדְּשֵׁי שְׁבִיעִי,
כֻּלָּם יִשְׂבְּעוּ וְיִתְעַנְּגוּ מִטּוּבֶךָ.
וְהַשְּׁבִיעִי רָצִיתָ בּוֹ וְקִדַּשְׁתּוֹ,
חֶמְדַּת יָמִים אוֹתוֹ קָרָאתָ,
זֵכֶר לְמַעֲשֵׂה בְרֵאשִׁית.

Yism'chu ישמחו

Text: **Shabbat Liturgy**

Music: **Traditional Chasidic**

Arranged by **Robbie Solomon**
Corresponding band arrangement by **Emily Tummons**

Corresponding band arrangement available in *Kol Han'shamah: Band Volume II* (TMP 994069)

Rubato ♩ = ca. 92
B
optional divisi
14
I
II
Shab - bat.
1. ah
2. ah
3. ah
m' - ka - d'- shei,
ra - tzi - ta - bo,
l' - ma - a - seih,
Shab - bat.
1. Am
(2.) i
3. Zei - cher
m' - ka - d'- shei m' -
ra - tzi - ta bo, ra -
l' - ma - a - seih, l' -
17
Shab - bat, ah,
Shab - bat, ah,
Shab - bat, ah,
ka - d'- shei sh' - vi - i, Shab - bat, ku - lam
tzi - ta bo v' - ki - dash - to, Shab - bat, chem - dat ya -
ma - a - seih v' - rei - shit, Shab - bat, zei - cher l' -
20
Last time to Coda
Tempo I
tutti
yis - b' - u,
ya - mim,
l' - ma - a - seih,
Shab - bat.
Shab - bat.
yis - b' - u v' - yit - an - gu mi - tu - ve - cha, Shab - bat.
mim o - to ka - ra - ta, Shab - bat.
ma - a - seih l' -

C
Yis - m' - chu v' - ma - l - chu - t' - cha shom - rei, shom - rei, shom - rei Shab - bat v'-
Yis - m' - chu v' - ma - l - chu - t' - cha shom - rei, shom - rei, shom - rei Shab - bat v'-
1.
D.S.
2.
D.S. al Coda
ko - rei o - neg Shab - bat. Shab - bat.
ko - rei o - neg Shab - bat. 2. V'-hash - vi - Shab - bat.
CODA
Tempo I
D
Sha - bat. Yis - m'-chu v' - ma - l - chu - t'-cha
ma-a-seih v'-rei - shit, Sha - bat. Yis - m'-chu v' - ma - l - chu - t'-cha
shom - rei, shom - rei, shom - rei Shab - bat v' - ko - rei o - neg, Shab - bat.
shom - rei, shom - rei, shom - rei Shab - bat v' - ko - rei o - neg, Shab - bat.

38
I
Yis - m' - chu v' - ma - l - chu - t' - cha shom - rei, shom - rei,
II
Yis - m' - chu v' - ma - l - chu - t' - cha shom - rei, shom - rei,
41
I
molto rit.
shom - rei Shab - bat v' - ko - rei o - neg, Shab - bat.
II
molto rit.
shom - rei Shab - bat v' - ko - rei o - neg, Shab - bat.